Praise for
Virtual Monopoly

"Many business people know that intellectual property – patents, trade marks and copyright – is important, but few know why. Not only does this book set out to explain some of the basics of intellectual property and assess its importance in modern strategic planning, it challenges many of the traditional approaches of big business and contrasts how innovative and successful businesses can be built using an intelligent appreciation of the power of the virtual monopoly. This is a stimulating and thought provoking book."
Dr. Gordon Wright, Partner, Elkington and Fife
(former Director of Intellectual Property, Sanofi-Synthelabo)

"Business must make the most of its intellectual property assets. This book points the way. Both business people and professionals can learn much from the author's lively and original approach."
Tim Roberts, President, Chartered Institute of Patent Agents

"As intangible assets represent an increasing proportion of the value of enterprises in the digital information economy, maintaining competitive advantages relies more heavily on the ability to protect intellectual property. In his new book, Virtual Monopoly, Chris Pike provides a balanced view of these often-controversial issues with insights for both practitioner and regulator, making a valuable contribution to this important debate."
Edward Truch, Director, Knowledge Management Forum,
Henley Management College

VIRTUAL MONOPOLY

VIRTUAL MONOPOLY

Building an intellectual property strategy
for creative advantage—from patents to
trademarks, from copyrights to design rights

Christopher G. Pike

NICHOLAS BREALEY
PUBLISHING

LONDON

First published by
Nicholas Brealey Publishing in 2001

36 John Street
London
WC1N 2AT, UK
Tel: +44 (0)20 7430 0224
Fax: +44 (0)20 7404 8311

1163 E. Ogden Avenue, Suite 705-229
Naperville
IL 60563-8535, USA
Tel: (888) BREALEY
Fax: (630) 898 3595

http://www.nbrealey-books.com
www.virtualmonopoly.net

Library of Congress Cataloging-in-Publication Data

Pike, Christopher, 1967–
    Virtual monopoly : building an intellectual property strategy in the creative economy :
from patents to trademarks, from copyrights to design rights / Christopher Pike.
        p. cm.
    Includes index.
    ISBN 1-85788-284-9
    1. Intellectual capital. 2. Intellectual property. 3. Intangible property. 4. Monopolies.
5. Patents. 6 Trademarks. 7. Copyright. 8. New business enterprises--Management. 9.
New products--Law and legislation. I. Title.

HD53 .P55 2001
658.4--dc21

2001037664

ISBN 1-85788-284-9

British Library Cataloguing in Publication Data
A catalogue record for this book is available from the British Library.

Printed in Finland by WS Bookwell.

CONTENTS

FOREWORD

THE ECONOMY IS DUMBING UP. THE SIGNS ARE ALL AROUND. TRULY unique, differentiated, and downright innovative products and services are creating waves and promising great returns.

This creative upshift is happening with good reason. During the 1980s pretty much every company embraced quality; in the 1990s they reengineered their business processes and set up in-house knowledge (or, at least, information) systems. Doing things faster, smarter, and more reliably has become the expected norm; it no longer provides much by way of market excitement or sustainable advantage. Future gains will be incremental at best. The time has therefore come to stop tinkering with "in the box" company organization stuff and to start creating "out of the box," innovative product, service, and business concepts. Creative advantage has become the new Holy Grail.

With creative advantage goes the power to shake up tired old industries. Look no further than the Dyson vacuum cleaner, for example, which challenges our preconceptions of what a vacuum cleaner should be and do: those vibrant colors, that funky shape. There is no bag, but rather patented "dual cyclone" suction technology. And what of the industry response to Dyson's creative leap forward? Not waving— Electrolux responds with comparative advertising[1] painting the Dyson cleaner in a negative light—but drowning—Hoover introduces a me-too Vortex product that the UK courts[2] find to have infringed Dyson's dual cyclone patent. Creative advantage talks, the competition balks.

Here's the rub: On its own, creative advantage cannot form the basis for strong, sustainable business advantage. What really matters is the ability to build proprietary, exclusive business space around that creative advantage by establishing effective barriers to competition. Intellectual property, in the form of patents, trade marks, copyrights, and so on, is the most powerful mechanism for protecting creative advantage. The Dyson vacuum cleaner is a great product, but its sustained market success owes much to the patent on its core technology. The patent sealed in the creative promise by defining exclusive boundaries that the courts were prepared to enforce.

This book will show you how to power up your own creative advantage and establish strong, exclusive business spaces through the strategic use of intellectual property.

However, exclusivity is only part of the picture. Intellectual property has become a media hot topic. The business press sizzles with stories of patent madness, cybersquatting, brand warfare, and the "napsterization" of content. In focusing on battles and controversy, there is a risk of missing the more fundamental shifts at play, which are about more than legal rumpus. The truth is that in the face of increasingly fluid global markets shaped by digital networks and extreme buzz, companies are finding it necessary to create islands of proprietary exclusivity. These islands are not permanent, but they at least provide a company with some breathing space in which to glean returns on its investment in developing new products and services. Innovative mechanisms for enhancing those returns are also being formulated.

This book takes a radical look at the bigger picture. For the first time, the new economics of virtual monopoly is defined. Intellectual property acts as the enabling currency, thereby taking on a dynamic business character quite distinct from its dusty, legal existence of old. The new economics offers unrivaled flexibility in terms of company and relationship structures, business models, and opportunities for profit generation. These are explored in detail from the perspectives of both large and small companies. Virtual monopoly economics also enables wholly different types of company to be created, such as ARM and Scipher whose business models are centered entirely on intellectual property. These "intellectual property company" forms are groundbreaking, but they have at least one precedent in the form of Thomas Edison's Menlo Park "invention factory."

The new economics of virtual monopoly redefines the balance of power in relationships between established companies and upstart creative players. It allows genuinely original companies to beat (or just engage differently with) old-style companies that have access to capital and economies of scale, but that lack real creative spark or energy.

Consider, for example, the effort that Microsoft has invested in wooing small, cutting-edge games designers to provide games for its new Xbox console. Microsoft has access to vast development capital, but in the absence of quality games it knows that its console will fail. Conversely, talented games designers who occupy exclusive creative spaces (defined by brands and copyright) know that they can strike great deals with even the biggest players.

The new economics of virtual monopoly empowers the creative company. However, as with all sources of powerful advantage, there are challenges and risks. It is impossible to ignore the threat posed by business trends toward me-too, fast-follower, and copycat products, and in the extreme by Napster-like digital piracy. The trends exploit gaps in intellectual property protection—either product specific or inherent in the legal framework—that enable copyists and pirates to scavenge off the creativity of the true originals. On the other hand, it should not be forgotten that intellectual property gives rise to legally enforceable monopoly rights that can be used to be aggressive with competitors and exert control over markets. Abuses are possible in which powerful rights holders unduly control entire markets. Drug patenting in Africa is a particular point of sensitivity, for example.

This book discusses the new challenges and risks, in addition to the growing opportunities. It does not hold back in calling for a balanced approach and for the careful, responsible stewardship of virtual monopoly power. This is, after all, an era of creative advantage, not one of dumbed-down, old-style capitalism and corporate muscle.

The new era is one in which breakthrough creative advantage, combined with the strategic use of intellectual property, can deliver the promise of sustainable returns for any company, regardless of size. The rewards of the new economics of virtual monopoly are there for the taking: It is time for your company to get dumbed up too!

ACKNOWLEDGMENTS

This book has been shaped and formed by the generous contributions of many. It is a pleasure to thank Nick Brealey and Sue Coll at Nicholas Brealey Publishing for their editorial feedback and guidance, particularly in helping to me to structure ideas and present them clearly. Above all, I thank them for taking a risk with an unpublished author in a subject area that at times seems to be mired in public controversy.

In large part, this book is the product of my practice experience in intellectual property. This started at Procter & Gamble, and I owe much to Tony Gibson for teaching me how to combat the complexities of patents law and practice. I am also grateful to him for tolerating my early forays into patent strategy. My early patent experiences were much influenced by Robin Hall. I remain indebted to his example of bullish inventiveness, ability to provide scientific rationale (and often data) to support legal argument, and for creating his folder named "patents." I also thank Robin and Senka for their recent hospitality during a book research trip to Beijing.

At GlaxoSmithKline, I owe much to the infectious enthusiasm and trusting approach of Hugh Dawson. I thank him for many discussions of the big picture, for his time in participating in an interview for this book, and for enabling me to work with GSK's Kiln devices design team. This is a team whose members genuinely live, eat, and breathe the quest for creative advantage. It has been a real pleasure building intellectual property positions that seek to do justice to their powerful design concepts. Particular thanks are offered to Stan Bonney for many stimulating conversations and for his participation in interviews. Thanks also to all the patent attorney team at GSK, including Helen Quillin for her continuing support, Andrew Teuten for review of various book drafts, Chuck Dadswell, Jim Riek, Chris Rogers, Annabel Beacham, and Berni Hambleton. Special thanks to Jessica Duhaney-Smith and Livia Haines for practical assistance.

At Pike & Co., I thank Jane Swift, Ian Bryan, Victoria Barry, and Jean Richardson for their assistance and above all patience during the preparation of this book. Thanks also to Matthew Blaseby for help in constructing the Virtual Monopoly website, www.virtualmonopoly.net.

Particular thanks to Maureen George at Henley Management College for the opportunity to present seminars on the business uses of intellectual property. The contributions and feedback of Henley MBA students over the years have helped me test and formulate my views. It is also a pleasure to recognize the support of the new Marlow mafia, particularly Giles Thrush and Ian Hinckley for their business advice and strategic lunches.

Many people have let me interrupt their busy lives so that I might learn from their experiences of intellectual property. I thank Mandy Haberman for sharing her story of establishing a one-person intellectual property company. Her leakproof Anywayup cup design remains a godsend for parents of toddlers everywhere. Thank you to Mike Muller at ARM Holdings for insights into how it all works in the IT industry and for convincing me of the power of the ARM intellectual property business model. I thank Quentin Vaile, Peter Ross, and Alan Sharp of Scipher for helping me take on board the dramatic intellectual property-centered birth of that company. I particularly thank Hilary Anderson for sharing her experiences as a signature creative in an industry in which the intellectual property regime does not always adequately support true originals.

Many others have also provided review input of draft versions of the book. I thank Luke Kempton at Wragge & Co. for input on business models; Jerome Spaargaren of Electronic IP for many "out of the box" comments; Nigel Roberts for recent examples in the detergent industry and for reminding me to keep it practical and relevant; Andrew Richards for perspective and overview; and Mark Ley for sociological insight.

Above all, I thank my parents, Edmund and Barbara Pike, and my sisters Angela, Julia, and Elizabeth for their support, kindness, and love. Without them I wouldn't have got this far.

PART ONE

THE NEW ECONOMICS OF
VIRTUAL MONOPOLY

1

FROM CREATIVE ADVANTAGE

TO VIRTUAL MONOPOLY

T HIS CHAPTER INTRODUCES THE NEW ECONOMICS OF VIRTUAL MONOPOLY. Its central theme is that building virtual monopoly by applying intellectual property to creative advantage can give rise to surprising business returns. Before we get into the detail, let me invite you to use your imagination.

THE MOST DESIRABLE BUSINESS SPACE IMAGINABLE

Close your eyes and try to conceive of a world in which your business owns and has exclusive access to the most desirable business space imaginable. That space is differentiated, wildly profitable, and enables you to create extraordinary shareholder value. Above all, the space is exclusively yours.

Now open your eyes and think of a current, real-life example. Possibly, you are thinking of Coca-Cola or Microsoft or Intel or Starbucks or another hugely valuable brand. Or maybe you are thinking of the exclusive technology space occupied by a major technology standard such as Windows, digital video disc (DVD), or Bluetooth. You may even be thinking of children's fiction sensation Harry Potter and the potential for royalty returns on book sales, not to mention character merchandising and film rights.

All of the above examples are differentiated and desirable business spaces. They are all based on a strong and highly marketable creative advantage in the form of a brand, technology, or content. But the fundamental reason that these spaces are capable of giving rise to extraordinary returns is their exclusive nature. All are protected by intellectual property that provides their owners with legal monopoly rights assertable against intruders. Coca-Cola, Microsoft, Intel, and Starbucks are trade marks. Patents protect the component parts of licensed technology standards. The Harry Potter books are subject to copyright.

In the absence of the exclusivity provided by intellectual property, the value of these business spaces would be severely diminished. Just think of the value of the brand name Coca-Cola in the absence of trade mark protection. Or, indeed, consider whether technology standards business models could exist at all without patents.

THE THREE COMPONENTS OF VIRTUAL MONOPOLY

Having challenged your imagination, let us return to some basics. There are three components of virtual monopoly:

◆ *Virtual monopoly* — the desired economic space
◆ *Intellectual property* — the tool for achieving that desired economic space
◆ *Creative advantage* — the starting point for intellectual property.

Virtual monopoly is the exclusive business space created when intellectual property is applied to creative advantage. The term "virtual" reflects the intangible character of intellectual property and the often temporary nature of the relevant monopoly position. Patents, design rights, and copyrights have a finite lifetime and trade marks must be used in trade if their legal monopoly substance is to be sustained. Monopoly is an old economic concept, characterized by exclusive and/or dominant market positions, high barriers to entry, premium pricing, and little or no effective competition. While monopoly requires careful regulation, the exclusivity that goes with it undoubtedly represents a highly desirable position for any business. Exclusive market presence, high competitive barriers to entry, premium pricing, and little or no competition—this is the stuff of a business person's dreams!

Monopoly can, of course, be based on many things, some of which are bad for competition, bad for the economy, bad for everybody. Abusive monopolistic behaviors based on aggressive market dominance, bullying of smaller competitors, price fixing, or other anticompetitive activities are not being advocated here. These practices restrict competition, distort the market, and adversely affect the consumer who faces higher prices and less choice. Virtual monopoly based on intellectual property granted by governments to protect creative advantage is altogether different.

Intellectual property systems encourage investment in creativity by rewarding the creative with legal monopoly rights that can be used to build exclusive spaces. Virtual monopoly based on intellectual property has for many years played a role, often a low-key one, in encouraging creative business and rewarding successful innovation. The growing importance of intellectual property reflects the new era of creative advantage that is shaping today's business landscape.

Intellectual property is a family of legal rights, including patents, trade marks, design rights, and copyrights, that form the currency for achieving virtual monopoly. As with any property right, intellectual property provides a legal monopoly right to exclude others from something that you own. In the context of virtual monopoly, that something is your creative advantage: a technology, a design, a brand concept. Some of the nuances of intellectual property are explored in the next chapter. For now, think of intellectual property as the legal right to control access to the commercial benefits of your creative advantage. That legal property right will naturally also have title (i.e., a defined owner) and be exploitable as a property asset by such means as sale or licensing.

MORE THAN A KNOWLEDGE ECONOMY

Now that the new economic concept of virtual monopoly has been introduced, let me at once draw a distinction between it and the currently fashionable knowledge economy model. In the knowledge economy, unique information and knowledge are strategic assets. This sounds great—until you start to think about how to protect and safeguard unique information and knowledge. We live in an increasingly interconnected world of digital systems, strategic alliances, virtual working, chat rooms, and portfolio careers. This is a world where information, knowledge, and indeed people flow readily and where safeguards against that flow are very difficult, perhaps even impossible, to establish. The knowledge economy is an inherently fluid landscape.

A practical example: Imagine that you are a major consumer products company seeking to develop a revolutionary new laundry product based on a unique understanding of consumer needs. You invest millions of dollars in consumer research by a marketing consultancy, which results in the Holy Grail of a genuine insight into what consumers want. How are you going to protect that insight, that unique knowledge of consumer needs? If you are wise you will initially give it a code name and only divulge it to key team members on a "need to know" basis. However, if you are going to build a business concept around this insight, you are going to need to open it up progressively to a wider audience. Your formulation technologists are going to need the details in order to get to work on formulating a product. The senior management team will have to be updated to get their buyin to funding the project. Marketing, purchasing, and manufacturing operations will all soon want the information.

Now think about your company, which you might once have regarded as a confidential, even safe environment. Think about all those consultants your company works with, including the marketing consultancy that did the initial research. Think about development partners, strategic alliances, and open supply chains. Think about employee churn rate and about how many of your ex-employees seem to end up working for competitors. Take it from me, that insight will seep, spread by osmosis, or otherwise wiggle its way out; give it three months, or six months at a stretch.

In any view of the economy, unique knowledge and insight are only strategic assets when they are under your control. Once you lose that control their competitive value is reduced, perhaps even to zero. The anti-intellectual property crusaders of the open source software movement (e.g., Linux) have got it right in at least one respect: Knowledge is free. Even business insight that was expensive to create can become valueless if it is not protected very carefully.

Virtual monopoly builds on but transcends and ultimately rejects the knowledge economy model, because the latter assigns far too much economic value to bare information and knowledge. This is readily demonstrated by the above "old economy" example. For even starker instances, think about all those dotcom failures that assigned value (in retrospect, too much value) to web traffic information, customer signup knowledge, and buzzy click-space insights rather than to any unique and proprietary differentiators.

The new economics of virtual monopoly regards information, knowledge, and insight as fluid entities, which are difficult to tie down and easily lost in an increasingly weblike, digital world. But virtual monopoly "fixes" unique knowledge, information, or insight-based creative advantage by way of intellectual property, which protects the differentiated technology, brand, design, or content. Virtual monopoly thereby rescues insight from a fluid, fragile knowledge economy existence and brings it into the well-defined and legally enforceable framework of intellectual property. Or at least it virtually does so, because intellectual property protects only the insight-derived creative advantage (e.g., the patented detergent product) as opposed to the insight itself (e.g., the consumer need).

CHARACTERISTICS OF VIRTUAL MONOPOLY

There are three defining characteristics of virtual monopoly: control of access, new kinds of buy–sell relationships, and moving from knowledge to property.

CONTROL OF ACCESS

Virtual monopoly gives you the opportunity to control access to your business space. Put simply, the owner of a virtual monopoly controls a non-open access, exclusive monopoly economic space. In opposing scenarios, that owner may choose to operate as the sole player in that space or to permit access on the basis of a licensing model.

As an example of the first scenario, think about the virtual monopoly space created by a patent for a global blockbuster drug such as Pfizer's Viagra for the treatment of male erectile dysfunction. The drug is a highly profitable product that many generic pharmaceutical companies would like to be able to sell. However Pfizer, which owns the patent for the drug molecule and the trade mark Viagra, will naturally want strict control over access to that virtual monopoly space and to those profits. Once the patent expires the space may open up, but for now unique access is the primary economic benefit provided by the patent, a virtual monopoly position.

Of course, the drug company could also play this the other way and adopt an open access licensing model. Indeed, this option is being debated as a means of ensuring that state-of-the-art Aids treatments reach Africa and the rest of the developing world. Control over access does not necessarily mean putting up the shutters. And, as we shall explore later, one emerging paradox of virtual monopoly is that more intellectual property can actually mean *enhanced* access because of the increasing attractiveness of licensing business models.

NEW KINDS OF BUY–SELL RELATIONSHIPS

Virtual monopoly gives rise to fundamentally different kinds of buy–sell relationships. In classical economics, that of Adam Smith for example, if a physical object — say, an orange — is sold the seller ceases to own it. In legal terms, the seller's property rights are exhausted. The buyer can, in general, do with the orange as they choose: eat it, juice it, plant its seeds, or whatever. Having sold the orange, the seller has made their sale and must find other things to sell to make further profit.

Conversely, in the knowledge economy model, if an idea — say, a technology for growing better oranges — is sold or utilized in the market for profit, the idea (i.e., the bare knowledge) is retained by the seller. The idea is still therefore available for further use or commercialization by the seller. But of course, once the idea is public and made available for the reworkers and recyclers, its value will be diminished. When it is widely distributed, the resale value of the idea may fall to zero.

Finally, in the virtual monopoly economy, a technology (probably derived from research knowledge) for growing better oranges may be protected by suitable intellectual property such as a patent. The technology may also have a brand name, for example "o-gro," and that name will be protected by a trade mark. The branded technology can be utilized by the owner or offered for sale from a virtual monopoly position enabling multiple usage and sales with little diminution of value. In fact, as the technology becomes better known the value of the patents and trade marks may well be enhanced. The economics of virtual monopoly therefore enables multiple transactions around the fruits of creativity with less potential for value loss—rather, with potential for value gain—over time.

FROM KNOWLEDGE TO PROPERTY

Virtual monopoly gives rise to the opportunity to establish defined intellectual property rights using knowledge, insight, and creativity as the starting point. Once created, intellectual property can be dealt with commercially, as with any other property. Increased opportunities for generating financial return are thereby established. The rights may, for example, be sold off as distinct property or be licensed on an ongoing royalty basis.

This characteristic is important, since the intellectual property value of many established companies outstrips that of their traditional assets based on real property: land, buildings, and machinery. Furthermore, there is a growing trend for many smaller, emerging companies in various industry sectors to use creative advantage as their prime model for establishing business value. Intellectual property provides a mechanism for safeguarding and liberating that value.

WHY VIRTUAL MONOPOLY IS SO RELEVANT

It goes without saying that today's economy is a complex and difficult place in which to operate. Many established business models for success have relied on identifying and capturing positions of unique sustainable advantage and exploiting the resulting financial returns. However, an emerging truth hitting many areas of industry and commerce is that unique sustainable advantage is becoming increasingly difficult to find and capture. Virtual monopoly is relevant because it provides a new and flexible source of at least temporarily sustainable advantage.

The dumbed-up economy has four defining features, each of which accentuates the demand for a new economics of virtual monopoly.

ACCESS

The economy is larger, more open, more global, and more accessible than ever before. Barriers to entry in almost all areas of commerce are falling, particularly in areas where digital and web technology can be employed. This economy of "open access" has the potential to give rise to advantage from the standpoint of size of market and volume of sales.

However, there are also more players with more ground to cover and fewer places to hide. More competition may mean lower margins. Different competitors may mean learning different rules. As many global businesses are finding out to their cost, sustainable advantage is not guaranteed just because the market is larger, more open, and more accessible.

BUZZ

The economy is faster and buzzier. The communications revolution means that information, ideas, and opinions can be shared more quickly. Product and service development teams interact globally using phone, email, video links, and web technology. Customer and supplier relationships are built up based on computer networks that enable real-time sharing of information. Informal networks develop around internet chat rooms, special-interest bulletin boards, or sharing of jokes and gossip via email.

The buzz is the sound of all this sharing of information, a 24/7 phenomenon. Buzz means that speed to market can be reduced, costs driven out, new relationships built, and existing relationships enhanced. Buzz also means that price, salary, product, and, indeed, company information can be shared quickly and largely uncontrollably. Opinions will be aired and confidential insights will leak out to your competitors, so buzz is a potential risk factor as well as a possible source of advantage.

CREATIVITY AND DIFFERENTIATION

Creativity and differentiation (C&D) are being advanced as a way of providing business with that elusive source of sustainable advantage. For example, *Business Week* heralds the "creative economy" as the business space for the twenty-first-century corporation.[1] "Differentiate or die" is the message of a recent business book.[2] Can C&D live up to expectations?

I believe so, and the reason for my belief can be found in any supermarket, in any shopping mall, or in any TV schedule. Each presents essentially the same experience. There is an illusion of product diversity and choice—many varieties, many flavors, many shop fronts, many channels—but there is little to get excited about and little true differentiation. This is the result of an economy in which any genuinely new ideas can be rapidly reworked and reapplied. Both access and buzz enable this recycling process.

Think about "animal-friendly cosmetics" or "West Coast coffee shops" or "organic foods" or "men's lifestyle magazines." Once applied in one place new ideas become available for recycling in other market spaces, perhaps even globally. They soon become generic, commonplace, and even dull. The challenge is then to sustain and protect creative advantage in the face of the reworkers and recyclers. This is where virtual monopoly comes into play to stop the reworkers and recyclers in their tracks. In short, virtual monopoly is based on good, old-fashioned exclusivity.

EXCLUSIVITY

Exclusivity based on intellectual property is as important now as it was to the nineteenth-century entrepreneurs. Their technology revolution founded on electricity, the railroad, and the telephone was accompanied by almost frenzied patenting of technology. Thomas Edison, the great American inventor of the time, filed more patents than anybody ever before (or since) and vigorously asserted and defended the resultant exclusive business spaces. The need for exclusivity in today's open access, dynamic, buzz economy has, however, become much, much greater. In an economy of "me too," "fast followers," and lookalikes in all shapes and forms, the exclusivity and non-open access character of virtual monopoly come as a breath of fresh air.

Business is starting to catch hold of this and patent filings worldwide are at their highest ever level. The battles have also started. The business press is alive with stories of business method patents, cybersquatting, and the "napsterization"[3] of the digital landscape. Exclusivity based on intellectual property is back on the business agenda as a source of advantage for the prepared and a source of risk for the unwary.

The reality is that while almost all large companies engage in intellectual property, only a leading few use it strategically to leverage the full advantages of virtual monopoly. This book will help you to join the leaders. In the next chapter, the basics of intellectual property — the currency of virtual monopoly — are introduced in more detail. Once you have the basics on board, we can start getting more deeply into the new and surprising business models of virtual monopoly.

2

THE CURRENCY OF

VIRTUAL MONOPOLY

INTELLECTUAL PROPERTY IS THE CURRENCY OF VIRTUAL MONOPOLY. IT ADDS legal force to creative advantage to bring the new economics of virtual monopoly into play. Intellectual property is also, of course, an area of law that can be complex to apply in detail. Throughout the first two parts of this book, I unapologetically concentrate on the business aspects of intellectual property. This inevitably means dispensing with some of the finer points of law in order to focus on the bigger picture. The third part of the book provides "tools" for building virtual monopoly and includes a few more of the practical legal details.

INTELLECTUAL PROPERTY AND CREATIVE ADVANTAGE

Three main forms of intellectual property comprise the principal currency of virtual monopoly:

◆ Patents—which protect technology advantage
◆ Trade marks—which protect brand advantage
◆ Copyright—which protects content advantage.

There are also subsidiary components to the currency in the form range of minor types of intellectual property, such as:

- ◆ Utility models — which protect (minor) technology advantage
- ◆ Design rights — which protect industrial designs
- ◆ Semiconductor mask rights
- ◆ Plant and animal variety rights
- ◆ Company names
- ◆ Internet domain names
- ◆ Database rights.

These subsidiary rights tend either to provide weaker protection or to be highly industry specific. For example, semiconductor mask rights are important to the IT industry, but are less important in other areas. Company names and internet domain names provide a degree of protection against users of essentially identical names, but lack the breadth and strength of trade marks. By contrast, the power trio of patents, trade marks, and copyrights have wide industry relevance and real strength.

PATENTS

Patents protect new and inventive (non-obvious) technology advantage. Both high- and low-technology advances are protectable, assuming that the basic requirements for novelty and non-obviousness are met. To give some examples, the technology may comprise a new dyestuff molecule, a detergent formulation, a leak-free diaper, a telecommunications switch apparatus, or a useful gene sequence. Some patents are filed on basic, fundamental technologies, but most patents cover improvements to existing technologies or new uses of technologies that are already known and used in other fields. The Dyson dual cyclone vacuum cleaner technology is, for example, supposed to have been inspired by a sawmill cyclone apparatus.[1] Patents generally confer 20 years' legal monopoly.

TRADE MARKS

Trade marks protect distinctive brand advantage. Distinctive words, logos, and in some countries even shapes, sounds, and smells may be registered. As examples of word trade marks, think of Intel, Nokia, Marlboro, Dr. Pepper, and Pampers. As examples of logo trade marks, think of the McDonald's golden arches, the Windows flying toaster, or Michelin's Monsieur Bibendum character.

Trade marks are registered against a defined specification of goods and services. That is why it is possible for the same mark to be used by different companies for different products. An example is the mark Polo, which is used for clothing (Ralph Lauren), cars (Volkswagen), and candy (the "mint with the hole," a slogan that is also a trade mark). Good trade marks are distinctive, readily recognizable, and immensely valuable differentiators in a crowded marketplace. Even more importantly, trade marks can confer an indefinite monopoly if the mark is used continuously in the course of trade.

COPYRIGHT

Copyright protects original literary, dramatic, artistic, and musical works (i.e., content) from the acts of copiers. Copyright is subtly different from patents and trade marks, which provide absolute legal monopoly rights that apply even where there is no intentional act of copying. Patents and trade marks can therefore be asserted against accidental, unintended, or "innocent" infringements. Copyright, on the other hand, requires copying; "independent creation" of the protected work is a defense to a copyright action.

Regardless of the legal subtleties, copyright is the dominant form of intellectual property in whole swathes of industry, from publishing to website design, from music to the performing arts, from films to computer programs. Copyright even protects product packaging and advertising. No registration of copyright is required, the rights generally coming into existence on recording of the work, although in a few countries, such as the US, copyright works may also be deposited with a government registrar. Copyright has a long lifetime, typically greater than 70 years.

COMBINING INTELLECTUAL PROPERTY FOR ADDED CURRENCY

Even from that brief introduction, you will appreciate that intellectual property offers a diverse and flexible currency for protecting different types of creative advantage. A fundamental part of building virtual monopoly rests in strategically mixing and matching the diverse kinds of intellectual property to ensure maximum protection.

By way of example, and with no pun intended, let us consider the well-known Monopoly board game. The game itself was patented back in the 1930s as US Patent No. 2,026,082,[2] although that patent has long since expired. The word MONOPOLY, by contrast, remains a registered trade mark for board games and the like in many countries. Other aspects of the game including the logo, a figure with a top hat and mustache, and the general "getup" of the box may also be trade marks and will certainly be subject to copyright. The board on which the game is played, the graphic design on the box cover, and even the play money are artistic and literary works for which copyright also subsists. The rulebook is a literary work that is subject to copyright. Since there are many variations of the game, including different language variations, different copyrights of potentially different scope and remaining lifetime will exist worldwide. The playing figures (boot, dog, car, and so on) are three-dimensional objects for which design protection may have been relevant. And no prizes for guessing what you'll find if you visit the website with the domain name www.monopoly.com. There is just as much value in having an exclusive address in internet space as there is in a game of property development.

Even a relatively familiar product can thus be protected by combining different types of intellectual property to create a strong, defensible virtual monopoly space. The exclusive nature of that space acts as a barrier to entry for copiers and safeguards the return on investment made in developing the product and nurturing the brand.

A CURRENCY OF LEGAL SUBSTANCE

Intellectual property, the currency of virtual monopoly, has legal character and substance. This means that, unlike bare knowledge and creative advantage, intellectual property provides:

◆ Defined scope of property
◆ Defined ownership of rights
◆ Enforceable rights of legal monopoly.

The legally defined and enforceable character of intellectual property makes it a transparent and straightforward way to tie down, manage, and deal commercially in creative advantage. In short, defined intellectual property is much more substantive and less fluffy to handle as a business currency than are bare knowledge and creativity.

As an example, let us imagine that you are a startup with a smart technology, say, for water purification. You need funding to take things forward and are considering either venture finance or a joint development agreement with a large multinational. Are you likely to be more successful if (a) you present yourself as a "knowledge company" with technology insight; or (b) you present yourself as a company holding patent applications for the defined aspects of your technology, well-documented design drawings for your apparatus (subject to design copyright), and a distinctive brand name and logo, both trade marked; plus, of course, knowledge and insight as well? The answer is plain: Approach (b) will make any funding proposal simpler to write and make the subsequent funding agreement easier to negotiate from a position of strength. The reason for this is merely that the intellectual property defines the relevant creative advantage in a way that is fixed, transparent, and amenable to commercial analysis.

Another example is ARM Ltd of Cambridge, UK, whose business is the design of microprocessors that form the brains for microchips used in a whole range of electronic devices, from mobile phones to electronic cameras to personal data assistants. Products incorporating the company's microprocessor design architectures are sold by the likes of Intel, Ericsson, Fujitsu, Motorola, Philips, and Sharp. In some ways, ARM is a classic "knowledge company," since its output is the knowledge behind the microprocessors. It makes no chips or devices itself. Most of its income is from licensing the microprocessor products.

I asked Mike Muller, the company's Chief Technology Officer, why it filed patents and generally placed emphasis on intellectual property. One of the principal reasons he gave was that the patents and other associated intellectual property gave legal substance to the company's licensing agreements. In other words, the intellectual property defines the technology substance of the license in a concrete way that knowledge alone never could do.

A CURRENCY FOR SAFEGUARDING INVESTMENT RISK

One of the biggest risks that any creative company runs is that time, money, and resources are invested in developing a new product or service, which is then copied or mimicked by competitors. The return on that investment in creativity gets eaten away. Intellectual property offers a way to safeguard against this situation through strong legal remedies against infringers.

A clear example is provided by the pharmaceutical industry. A new drug entity typically takes 8–12 years' development time and $300–500 million in investment to bring to the market. No pharmaceutical company could justify making that investment without the legal reassurance provided by the patent on the drug molecule. It will come as no surprise that pharmaceutical companies are fervent defenders of their patents against infringers.

Creative startup companies with products or services requiring development investment are further equally strong examples. Many companies of this type are established by entrepreneurs who, in the early stages, invest their own savings in the creative product. Some even remortgage their home to liberate early-stage development capital. For them, a pending patent or even a trade mark application provides at least some reassurance that their great idea will not be stolen from underneath their noses. The patent or trade mark is also useful at a later stage in negotiations with potential investors or licensees. Intellectual property safeguards their investment as creative entrepreneurs.

Another major risk for any creative company is that the market intro-duction of a new product or service is blocked by a competitor's intel-lectual property. The likelihood of this scenario resulting in a major block is reduced if the creative company stakes its claim first by pre-emptive filing. The very act of being first to establish intellectual prop-erty in a particular business space makes it more difficult for competing third parties to obtain broad rights in that area. And even if a competi-tor does obtain some sort of position, the existence of earlier, pre-emptive rights is likely to provide at least a bargaining position. For example, when a patent is applied for to protect a technology, the patent application is published 18 months after filing. Publication brings the technology into the public domain and thereby makes it less likely that a third party will be able to obtain broad, blocking patent rights in the same area.

A CURRENCY OF BUY–SELL RELATIONSHIPS

Business is all about buy–sell relationships, for which intellectual prop-erty is becoming a major currency. Think about the following:

◆ Employees
◆ Consultants
◆ Development and franchise partners
◆ Strategic alliance partners.

While they have differing characteristics and objectives, all these busi-ness relationships are ultimately buy–sell relationships. They involve softer assets such as time, skills, resources, contacts, and knowledge, but they are nonetheless buy–sell relationships. Intellectual property will be part of the relationship, as an explicit component, a hidden component, or a potential outcome.

As one example, a technology company will certainly want to ensure that any patents arising from work done by employees and consultants belong to the company. When setting up development partnering and strategic alliances, all parties will be using their intellectual property to leverage better financial and access terms. Ownership of relevant background intellectual property probably even influences the initial selection of those development and alliance partners.

However, let me take things even further and ask you also to consider the buy–sell relationships with:

◆ Suppliers
◆ Distributors
◆ Customers.

Intellectual property can affect the terms of these buy–sell relationships as well. Imagine that you are a toy maker and you need to source certain electronic components for a new electronic talking bunny. The components may be of an entirely generic nature, in which case you are likely to make the sourcing decision on the basis of reliability of supply, quality, and above all price. However, the component may be more technology rich. In that case your sourcing decision is likely to be influenced by who owns, or has access to, the intellectual property on that component. The price will also be different.

Intellectual property has become a currency of the supply relationship. Some companies are going so far as to make that quite explicit. In a recent article, IBM claims to have used its intellectual property to leverage "more than $30 billion in components and product deals for its technology group in 1999."[3]

What of buy–sell relationships with distributors and customers? Here intellectual property affects price. Why does a can of Pepsi cost more than a can of supermarket own-brand cola? The answer mainly lies in the Pepsi trade mark. Why does a movie on DVD cost more than the same movie on VHS? In part, it is due to the the size of the royalty paid to the consortium that owns the patent-protected DVD technology. Intellectual property is there as part of the currency of the buy–sell relationship across the entire supply chain.

A CURRENCY OF BUSINESS MODELS

If intellectual property is becoming a currency of buy–sell relationships, can it also be used as the currency for business models? It can. The next two chapters are about virtual monopoly business models based on intellectual property.

For now, let me firmly emphasize that intellectual property is a creature of property. This means that it can be used in business terms in much the same way as traditional "bricks and mortar" property. The property may be bought and sold. Mortgages may be obtained. Licenses or franchises may be granted and rent collected in the form of royalty payments. Property portfolios may be established and managed to develop portfolio value over and above their individual component parts.

However, the virtual nature of intellectual property means that new and different kinds of business models based on property exploitation are made available. For example, in the bricks and mortar world you could not, for example, rent out a property to more than a limited number of tenants. Microsoft, by contrast, has hundreds of millions of licensees for the copyright on its Windows operating system. In effect, a new copyright license comes into force each time the shrinkwrap is removed from a newly acquired Windows CD.

A CURRENCY FOR MEASURING CREATIVE ADVANTAGE

A further subtle but important use of intellectual property is to provide an independent metric for the quality and substance of creative output. The patent system, which protects technology advantage, provides a good example of this. To be capable of patent protection a technology must be both new and inventive over anything published anywhere in the world before the filing date of the patent. Obtaining grant of a patent following independent examination by the Patent Office is therefore a good measure that your technology is both new and inventive, although this is to an extent limited by the degree of thoroughness of the relevant Patent Office examination. The independent "seal of approval" provided by patent grant can be used in marketing the product. For example, the grant number of the patent may be applied to the product as an indication of its technical uniqueness. That product marking also serves to warn others that the technology behind the product is proprietary to the patent owner.

The independent quality check can also be useful in the corporate environment. As Stan Bonney, manager of GlaxoSmithKline's Innovative Device Concepts group, commented:

> *"We see the grant of patents relating to our drug delivery device concepts as providing a good external indicator of the quality of our device design capabilities."*

He also mentioned that merely filing a patent has some significance:

> *"I appreciate that filing patents is not an inexpensive business and that our attorneys are therefore selective about what we choose to patent. The fact that the company chooses to invest in patenting our device concepts is an indicator both of the company's belief in the commercial value of our design work and in our attorneys' belief in the originality of what we do."*

He then went on to explain how he sometimes uses the filing of a patent as part of the marketing effort he employs to "sell" new device concepts to the company as a whole:

> *"If our commercial people know that a patent has been filed and I can say that our attorneys are confident of patent grant, this is good independent evidence of the quality of the overall device design offering."*

It goes without saying that similar "sales" techniques can be used by startup firms to help win over potential investors.

INTELLECTUAL PROPERTY IS BECOMING A GLOBAL CURRENCY

The emergence of the global economy has been well documented. Creative advantage is naturally a creature of the global economy—or, rather, creativity respects no boundaries. For example, the advance of the internet and the digital telecommunications revolution form a global phenomenon, just as the music of the Beatles or the Rolling Stones did 30 years previously.

Unfortunately, until quite recently the laws of intellectual property were not at all aligned globally. With some exceptions, intellectual property could be fairly characterized as a ragbag collection of national laws and procedures, with some harmonization along traditional political, regional, or possibly colonial lines, but with immense variation even between neighboring countries.

For example, up until 1994 the Coca-Cola Company could not register the shape of its bottle as a trade mark in the UK, despite owning corresponding registrations in other countries of the European Union. As another example, if somebody in the early 1970s claimed to have a world patent on a technology, you could with justification laugh in their face. Not only is there no such thing as a world patent, but at that time obtaining patent protection in many countries was a practical and bureaucratic nightmare. The old world of intellectual property was a complex, costly minefield that was incredibly difficult, if not impossible, to manage along global lines.

However, things are changing. The main trends are the following.

GLOBAL HARMONIZATION OF INTELLECTUAL PROPERTY LAWS

International standards for patents, designs, trade marks, and copyright law were agreed under the auspices of the Trade Related Aspects of Intellectual Property Rights (TRIPS) agreement.[4] The vast majority of countries have now brought their law into line with TRIPS, or are in the process of doing so. For example, China has recently aligned its laws with TRIPS as a precondition for joining the World Trade Organization.[5]

The TRIPS agreement also sets out basic international standards for enforcement of intellectual property rights, including enforcement against counterfeiting. Again, the vast majority of countries are bringing their law into line with TRIPS, although it is fair to say that practical experience remains patchy in those countries where most change was required.

GLOBAL AND REGIONAL HARMONIZATION OF REGISTRATION PROCEDURES

There are numerous examples of this kind of harmonization, many engendered by the World Intellectual Property Organization (WIPO) in Geneva. For example, the Patent Co-operation Treaty[6] and the Madrid Protocol[7] provide simplified procedures for obtaining patents and trade marks respectively on a multicountry basis. The Patent Law Treaty[8] (not yet in force) radically simplifies the legal formalities required to obtain a patent in different countries worldwide. Other harmonizing influences include those applied by the European Union, such as the Directive on the harmonization of trade mark laws.[9] The Directive was good news for Coca-Cola, which was eventually able to register the shape of its bottle as a trade mark in the UK.

EVOLUTION OF SUPRANATIONAL RIGHTS

There is now a Community Trade Mark, which is a single trade mark registration covering all member states of the European Union. The Community Patent and the Community Design also look to be on the horizon.

The .com domain name suffix is maybe the first truly global intellectual property right, although some would say that it is not global, but rather a US entity. The residents of Tuvalu, a small South Pacific island whose .tv domain name suffix has become hot property, would doubtless not shun the global description.

INTEGRATED PATENT OFFICE SYSTEMS AND FEE REDUCTIONS

Ten years ago all intellectual property procedures were paper based and the various national government intellectual property offices rarely communicated with each other. However, electronic procedures are starting to come on to the agenda. Interestingly, the larger Patent Offices (i.e., US, European Patent Office, and Japan) are beginning to integrate their office systems. Digital sharing of information is being enabled, which should cut out duplication of effort (e.g., in searching).

Harmonized, integrated, and supranational procedures can be cheaper to administer than separate, national ones. Combine this with recent deliberate (and political) lobbying from pressure groups for better-value services, and you start to get fee reductions at the Patent and Trade Mark Offices. For example, the European Patent Office has carried out a whole series of across-the-board fee reductions, which have made the always high-quality, but once expensive EPO procedures now seem good value. The simplification of procedures should also result in smaller attorney's fees for routine, bureaucratic tasks.

THERE IS STILL SOME WAY TO GO

There are strong harmonizing trends at force, but we are not yet at the stage of being able to apply for a global patent or global trade mark via a single electronic application. That day will come, but it will probably take 20–30 years if matters progress as rapidly as they are currently. What will push us toward that situation is the domain name registration experience. More and more clients ask me, "If I can register 'myname.com' instantly online for $100, why might it cost $50,000 plus to register MYNAME as a trade mark in 50 countries?" The question is a good one. Part of the answer is that while the procedures for trade mark registration are becoming more harmonized, many separate official and agents' fees in the various countries need to be paid to cover the different legal procedures. The other part of the response is that because trade marks are potentially more powerful kinds of intellectual property than domain names, it is right to have greater bureaucratic safeguards against the grant of broad rights.

There are also some major areas of intellectual property law and procedure that are not harmonized. For example, in court procedures there are broad and gaping differences between the inquisitorial procedures of the civil law countries of continental Europe, the adversarial procedures of the UK and the US, and the state bureaucratic procedures of the ex-communist countries. In patents, there are clear differences between the "first to invent" procedures of the US and the "first to file" procedures of almost every other country. The intriguingly named "interference proceedings," which delve into competing inventorship dates, are also a unique aspect of US patent practice. The desire for each EPO member state to require translation of granted European patents into its own local language is another peculiarity, although this looks to be on the way out.

WHAT DOES THE GLOBALIZATION OF INTELLECTUAL PROPERTY MEAN FOR BUSINESS?

Increasing global harmony in the area of intellectual property has a number of implications for business, the majority of them positive:

◆ *Global intellectual property portfolio development.* This is now possible. It is true that it continues to be bureaucratically complex, but the trend is toward simplification. It is also true that it can still require the payment of many local agents' fees and official fees, but cost pressures are downward.

◆ *Increased global certainty on portfolio value.* Substantive intellectual property laws are now harmonized. Predicting whether an intellectual property position will able to be established on a global basis for any particular technology, brand, or design concept is therefore more straightforward. The opportunity to leverage global value from creative advantage is also becoming more possible. The uncertainty of differing local legal factors has largely been taken out of the equation. However, poor enforcement and counterfeiting remain real threats in some countries.

◆ *Increased global certainty on risk factors.* Advanced search systems with global reach, including those available at minimal cost via the internet, make it more possible to assess intellectual property risk factors from a global standpoint. Furthermore, the harmonization of substantive intellectual property laws increasingly takes the uncertainty of differing local legal factors out of the risk assessment equation.

◆ *Possibility of global virtual monopoly economics.* Business models that seek to leverage the economics of virtual monopoly can become global in scale and outlook. Greater global recognition and respect of the value associated with intellectual property are the enabling factors. At a practical level, this may mean that a company chooses to exploit a technology or brand globally, or instead to exploit it directly in certain countries and license it in others. The range and scope of any exploitation or licensing model can be broadened because of more effective global protection. Poor enforcement of rights and counterfeiting in some countries are the remaining significant risk factors, but the opportunities for virtual monopoly business models on a global scale have become increasingly real.

3

FROM CURRENCY TO

BUSINESS MODEL

I T IS ONE THING TO USE INTELLECTUAL PROPERTY AS BUSINESS CURRENCY. IT is another to make it the cornerstone of your business model. This chapter explores the business models of virtual monopoly together with some supporting trends. The following chapter takes things even further by introducing companies that have embraced intellectual property so deeply that it has become their core reason for existence. These are the emergent "intellectual property companies."

THE BUSINESS MODELS OF VIRTUAL MONOPOLY

There are four principal business models based on virtual monopoly:

◆ Fortress monopoly
◆ Value-added monopoly
◆ Hub monopoly
◆ Monopoly-in-a-box.

The characteristics of the four models are distinct, although some companies are transitioning between models or attempting to run models in tandem. The models are open to companies that have already integrated the creation of intellectual property deeply with their business structures. These companies have developed vibrant and powerful virtual monopoly positions, which give them right of access to the new economics of virtual monopoly.

FORTRESS MONOPOLY

This model consists essentially of fortress-like virtual monopoly spaces built around desirable and highly profitable product or service entities. The spaces are impenetrable to outsiders other than by permission of the owner. Their legal basis comprises every applicable type of intellectual property right, particularly strong patents and/or trade marks, combining to form totally defensible virtual monopoly positions. The fortress may be further strengthened by product or service registration requirements, which only increase the already massive barriers to entry for outsiders.

While the fortress is secure, it is not immune from threats. The main threat to companies following this model is the "big cliff." This can, for example, be a major market shift that makes the fortress position no longer desirable. Or it can be a major legal or regulatory shift that renders the fortress position indefensible. A consequence of facing the "big cliff" is exposure to market competition in a way that these companies are just not used to. This may expose organizational bloatedness, since one consequence of sheltering under the umbrella of a fortress can be lax attention to cost and efficiency. If not managed with supreme care, the "big cliff" has the potential to push these companies into doomsday scenarios.

PHARMA, PERFUMES, AND PHOTOCOPIERS

The fortress monopoly is the dominant business model for big pharmaceutical companies. The current business models of companies such as Pfizer, Merck, AstraZeneca, and GlaxoSmithKline depend on blockbuster drug products protected by strong patent and regulatory exclusivity positions. R&D investment in these products is immense. The fortress monopoly model protects that investment and enables return on it to be generated by super-premium pricing in regulated markets. The threats of generic infringements, counterfeiting, and parallel imports are fought on an almost daily basis by these companies, all of whom have large inhouse legal teams. Antitrust can also be an issue, arising particularly in the context of mergers and acquisitions.

However, the "big cliff" for big pharma is represented by patent expiry. When the patent on a blockbuster drug expires, the fortress monopoly model breaks down, at least for that drug. Competition enters the market, pricing premia are reduced, and revenues potentially plummet. The principal strategy to date for managing patent expiry has been to ensure that there is a constantly regenerating pipeline of fortress monopoly-protected drugs, so that as one drug molecule faces the "big cliff" one or more others are coming onstream to replace lost revenue. Another post-"big cliff" strategy could involve transitioning into one of the other virtual monopoly business models described below.

Legendary perfume house Chanel also employs the fortress monopoly business model. This time it is based on the brand, or rather the trade mark CHANEL, which is internationally famous. Control over brand evolution and the marketing and sales environment is strict. Pricing is super-premium. This is certainly one of those products where people pay for the name, and indeed the name may be the most valuable product attribute. Threats to Chanel's business include counterfeiting and parallel imports, and any acts that reduce the company's control over the quality of the product and the way it is sold.

The "big cliff" threat for a company like Chanel is change of market sentiment, which may even be fashion driven. One strategy is to make a product like this entirely fashion proof. Another strategy is to build up a portfolio of fortress brands, much as LVMH now appears to be doing with Louis Vuitton, Moët & Chandon, Hennessy, and other famous brands. This reduces business exposure as a whole to changes in fashion, much as a broad-based drug development pipeline protects big pharma from patent expiry. One risk inherent in this strategy can be dilution of individual power brands if the elements of the portfolio are not managed with extreme care.

Xerox Corporation[1] provides a final example from history of the fortress monopoly model. In the 1960s and early 1970s its grip on the light lens copier market was almost total. Indeed, its presence was so strong that it had to fight to stop its trade mark, Xerox, from becoming a generic term for the act of making a photocopy. Xerox's position was protected by swathes of patents filed globally. At the time it was one of the very few companies that could contemplate the bureaucratic challenge of filing patents in upwards of 100 countries. Its organization was vertically integrated. Its tight control of the supply chain even extended to seeking to control exclusive supply of Xerox paper for use with Xerox copiers.

The "big cliff" for Xerox came in the form of antitrust. In 1975 a Federal Trade Commission consent decree required it to license its copier patents to competitors. Immediately, the market was flooded with cheaper Japanese low-volume copiers. Xerox's flabby and bureaucratic organization structure, built up under the protective umbrella of the fortress, meant that competing on cost and value terms was almost impossible. It retained positions in the prestige, high-volume copier market, but has never really recaptured lost share in cheaper, low-volume copiers.

VALUE-ADDED MONOPOLY

The value-added monopoly model is characterized by virtual monopoly spaces built to protect key value-adding features of the product or service. The objective is to block competitive access to those value-adding features, which can then be used as exclusive marketing points to support premium-priced offerings. Companies operating this model often sell on the basis of "new, improved X" or "now with added Y" value propositions. The spaces are defined by various types of intellectual property right, such as patents for value-added technology aspects, trade marks for value-added brand aspects, or copyright for value-added content aspects.

There is no single major threat to companies following the value-added monopoly model. There is no "big cliff," rather a succession of smaller hills to climb. These companies must keep developing new, improved, market-relevant, and protectable value-added features to stay ahead of the competition. Continuous innovation is required, because the barrier to entry posed by value-added features is only as strong as the market advantage arising from the exclusive presentation of those features.

CONSUMER PRODUCTS AND PUBLISHING

Strong market advantage can arise from a simple but exclusive value-added feature. Think about Procter & Gamble's Always feminine hygiene product, which in the 1980s was the first to incorporate the now ubiquitous "wings" technology. This unique and patented feature formed the basis for a highly effective marketing campaign that enabled Always to develop into one of the fastest established global mega-brands.

Indeed, value-added monopoly has become the model for consumer products. Go to any shelf or aisle of any supermarket and you will encounter the value-added monopoly model at play. Take the coffee section. The different brands will be protected by trade marks. The jars will not be arranged haphazardly on the shelves; there is a defined pecking order. The prime shelf positions are occupied by the brand leaders, who use their value-added monopoly to leverage their positions with the supermarkets. There is also a good chance that one or more of the coffee products is on special offer. More than likely it will be the brand leader that is being used as a "loss leader," that is, a product that is very keenly priced and advertised as such to attract people into the store. Combine these factors and you get a profit structure in consumer goods where the brand leader is much more profitable to its brand owner than the number two brand, which itself is much more profitable than the other brands. This profit structure is a direct consequence of the value-added monopoly model. Protected value-added features give the brand leader greater leverage, which in turn leads to greater profit opportunities.

Let us have another look at the coffee shelves. Spot the lookalike products, a major source of annoyance for the brand leaders. There will probably be quite a few of them, each borrowing one or more brand attributes of the leaders but not getting so close as to violate any intellectual property. Then look for the value-added technology. Possibly there are "fresh aroma" granules. There is probably some patented process technology there. Perhaps there are packaging innovations, which again will be patent protected. Maybe some jars have a distinctive shape, which is likely to be protected by a registered design. Any graphic design on the labels will be copyright protected. There is combination chemistry at play, combining different sorts of intellectual property to provide overall value-added monopoly spaces.

Book publishing is another area where value-added monopoly is at work. When I was looking for a publisher for this book I did quite a lot of research. I went to bookshops, large and small, in a number of countries and investigated which publisher commanded the best positions on the shelves. This gave me an idea which business book publishers had brand leverage with the booksellers. I also went to remainder bookshops. This gave me an idea which publishers' books were most often remaindered. I looked at my own bookshelf and tried to identify which publisher was responsible for publishing the most influential (to me) business books in the past five years. I considered print quality, flyleaf design, even the weight of the books, a key factor when choosing a book to read when traveling. I visited publishers' websites and the main online bookstores.

In short, I was looking not just at quality but also at value-added attributes and for a publisher that was leveraging its brand within the various sales and distribution channels. I wanted a publisher that knew how to operate a value-added monopoly model. Nicholas Brealey Publishing, my UK publisher, came out at the top of the list. At our first meeting, I was pleased to hear Nick tell me that the distinctive "nb shooting star" logo was protected by a trade mark. The company's effectiveness at operating the value-added monopoly model also meant that I offered it rights to this book first. It helped to initiate and seal the author–publisher relationship.

Microsoft operates a number of different virtual monopoly business models. Its ability to do this is one of its great strengths. Microsoft certainly operates value-added monopoly business models. For example, its Office 2000 product is not the only suite of office tools software on the market. It does, however, offer a value-added position by virtue of its brand, protected by various trade marks, and, by virtue of its software code, protected by copyright. This allows Microsoft to sell at a premium price and to leverage relationships with distribution and sales channels and develop customer loyalty. It is nevertheless innovating continually and has to compete with various me-too products. Counterfeiting, particularly in China, has been a well-known problem for Microsoft.

HUB MONOPOLY

The starting point for the hub monopoly model is a well-defined "hub" platform (e.g., a technology platform) that has many potential applications and that many companies will want to use in their own products or services. It is even better if it is an agreed technology standard such as an operating system or an industry standard research tool such as a database tool. The technology is primarily protected by patents, but other rights such as copyright for software aspects, mask right for chip design aspects, and database right for database aspects may be relevant. Hub access is offered, by way of licensing, to all comers, although key industry players may be offered preferential terms to encourage early adoption.

An important feature of the hub monopoly model is that the value of any particular hub will tend to increase with the number of licensees, end-users, and different uses to which the hub technology is applied. The economic theory of increasing returns,[2] as developed by Professor W. Brian Arthur of Stanford University and the Santa Fe Institute, very much applies. The more uses for and users of the technology, the potentially more valuable it becomes. Get a large enough base of uses and users and the whole thing can snowball on an increasing returns upward curve.

A simple example here is compact disc technology, which has found use as a storage medium for both recorded music and computer software, thereby increasing its user base and market potential. New uses of compact discs include mail-drop marketing campaigns to get people to sign up with particular internet service providers. How many CDs has AOL sent you in the past year? That kind of marketing can only work because the compact disc is a hub technology standard.

The main threat to the hub monopoly model is our old friend the "big cliff." This is in one instance a shift to a new hub technology, such as the shift from CD to DVD storage media. In another instance, this is a major legal or regulatory shift that removes or weakens the monopoly surrounding the hub technology, such as if a basic patent is found invalid. Other threats include infringements of the intellectual property rights to the hub technology, such as by clone makers or, indeed, counterfeiters.

TECH STANDARDS, GENE TOOLS, AND CHIP ENGINES

An early but immensely important example of the hub monopoly model concerns the US patent issued jointly to Stanford University and the University of California in San Francisco on Cohen and Boyer's technique for manipulating recombinant DNA.[3] The technique was fundamental to the emerging biotech industry, a true example of a research technique acting as a hub technology for many applications. At the time the patent was granted, the biotech industry was in its infancy and the law concerning biotech patents was not well established. Challenges to the validity of the patent might have been expected. These did not arise, for the good reason that the patent owners made the patent openly available for license to all. Modest licensing fees were charged to commercial groups and free licenses were granted to academic researchers. The biotech industry plugged into the business model, paid up, and used the technique as a building block for its future.

Another early and well-known example contrasting the fortress monopoly model with the hub monopoly model arose in the early days of domestic video recorders. There were two emerging standards, VHS and Sony's (reputedly superior) Betamax. Sony applied a fortress monopoly model and only allowed the Betamax standard to be used with its proprietary machines. The VHS standard, by contrast, was openly licensed as a technology hub and was therefore adopted by many manufacturers. Over time, VHS machines got better and cheaper and it became more difficult to find Betamax tapes. VHS won the standards battle. It possibly was not as good technically as Betamax, but the hub monopoly business model was more powerful.

There are numerous other examples of the hub monopoly model applied to technology standards. Bluetooth, the emerging wireless device communications standard, is one of these. Notice that with Bluetooth, branding is starting to come into play. Maybe soon we will be asking for a Bluetooth-enabled personal data assistant just as we ask for a PC with an Intel Pentium processor.

Celera Genomics is operating a leading-edge hub monopoly business model. This is the commercial entity that won the race to sequence the human genome[4] by investing in state-of-the-art gene sequencing and computational analysis tools. Celera Genomics has a complete database of the human genome available for license, and reputedly also has applied for 7,000 patents. In essence, it owns a fundamental technology hub into which all the key players in the biotech industry are likely to want to plug. In one aspect, the Celera licensing business model provides the big drug companies with subscriber access to its database hub. The recombinant DNA example mentioned earlier may offer the company a lesson from history, particularly in terms of public relations acceptance for the business model.

The Celera example already seems to be inspiring others in the biotechnology field. Athersys, a leader in proteomics, has developed the patented technique of random-activation gene expression (RAGE) as a way of inducing genes to produce proteins, the primary factors in disease and healing. This technique can be used to mine the genome databases now available for furthering advances in drug discovery. According to *Red Herring*[5] this could be set to become "the killer app for creating drugs." Athersys has reportedly already established access licenses with Medarex, Acorda Therapeutics, and Elan, and research collaborations with a number of medical schools and universities. Whether this is translated into a full hub monopoly business model built around a "RAGE hub" remains to be seen.

ARM wins my vote for best hub monopoly business model to date. Its business is the design of microprocessors that form the engines for chips used in a whole range of electronic devices, from mobile phones to electronic cameras to personal data assistants. It only designs, it makes no physical products at all. Mike Muller, the company's Chief Technology Officer, painted a picture of its business model for me:

"We design the [microprocessor] engines. The engines are, for example, protected by patents and semiconductor mask rights. We then license the engines to 40 or so chip makers. They pay us an upfront fee and also agree to pay small ongoing royalties for each chip they sell which uses our engine design. The engines are multipurpose. They can be used in chips for a whole range of applications from your lawnmower to your car dashboard to your mobile phone. Each chip manufacturer uses our engine design in maybe 100 or so different chips for use in various different products."

One engine design licensed to more than 40 chip makers, each of which uses it in 100 or so different chips for a range of product types. Can you see the ongoing royalties beginning to stack up? Can you also appreciate how ARM's risk in ongoing royalties is balanced over 40 licensees times 100 different products? This is a truly great business model.

One thing I particularly like about ARM's business model is that it is both jam today — in the form of the upfront fee — and jam tomorrow — in the form of ongoing royalties. There are also scones and cream, because ARM additionally provides technology consulting, systems development, and support services. The company is also starting to get into branding with its "ARM-powered" logo. Initially, its intent is to develop brand recognition within the chip development community. But, as Intel has shown with its "Intel Inside" logo, it is possible to build consumer brand recognition around high-tech components that are rarely seen by the consumer.

There is an interesting historical twist to the ARM story. The company's origins lie in the Acorn computer company, which was a small manufacturer of good-quality personal computers. That product-based business went through a rough patch until in 1990 it changed tack completely and went from making and selling computers to its current hub monopoly business model based on intellectual property. From seven people and a powerful business idea in 1990, it has a current workforce of around 600 (60 percent R&D staff) and a January 1, 2001 market capitalization of about $7.5 billion. And as they say in its marketing blurb, although you may never have heard of the company, you almost certainly own a product that is powered by an ARM-designed microprocessor.

MONOPOLY-IN-A-BOX

The starting point for the monopoly-in-a-box is similar to that for the hub monopoly, but the way revenue is generated is quite different. The monopoly-in-a-box model starts with a well-defined slice of creative advantage that has real commercial applications. That creative advantage must be attractive to at least one well-funded company that will want to use it in an identifiable product or service. It must also be protected by suitable intellectual property rights to form a defined virtual monopoly position. In this model, returns are generated through sale or exclusive licensing of the defined virtual monopoly position to a third party.

Notice the difference between this approach and that of the hub monopoly. Here the terms are exclusive, whereas in the hub monopoly model access to the hub is essentially open to anyone who is prepared to take a license. The creative advantage need not have hub character or even be generally desirable. It is enough that it is an attractive proposition to one well-funded third party.

DRUG DELIVERY SYSTEMS AND POP COSMETICS

The monopoly-in-a-box model is being employed by an ever greater number of specialist technology consulting firms, such as PA Technology Consulting. The consulting firm develops market expertise in a particular industry area and attempts to develop insight into which way the market is going. Creative advantage solutions that fit with the identified market trends are then developed. These are offered for sale or on an exclusive licensing basis to the large industry players. Even if a particular deal does not come off, the act of attempting to sell the solution to the large industry player may result in insider insight being acquired through a process of osmosis. This can be applied to generate tailored solutions. Innovation cash burn must be a major challenge for these companies. They often also do contract research and development or, indeed, offer management consulting services. This generates income and also helps build relationships with the industry players.

Another example of the monopoly-in-a-box model is the needleless injection drug delivery system developed by Powderject. This enables targeting of injectables to precise skin layers within the epidermis. Powderject has set up a number of development projects with large players in the pharmaceutical industry to investigate uses of the comprehensively patented technology in different therapeutic areas. A likely outcome for any particular successful project would be an exclusive product license to a big pharma company. In one scenario, the license would be restricted to a particular therapeutic area. Even if the project does not result in a licensing deal, Powderject potentially benefits by having had access to the development facilities of the larger company to test out its technology.

Powderject's business model is perhaps smarter than this brief description can credit. One of the more interesting aspects is that Powderject is branding its delivery system in a development of the "Intel inside" approach. According to the company's chief executive, Paul Drayson, its hope is that when offered a particular therapy by their doctor, patients will inquire, "Doesn't it come in a Powderject?"

A headline from an article in a recent edition of the *Financial Times*[6] — "Cosmetic giants look to collar wave of start-ups" — documents a growing trend within the cosmetics industry for big players such as L'Oréal to attempt to acquire small but successful new brand entrants. Often the new brand entrant is bought lock, stock, and barrel. The *Financial Times* article highlights the risks of this acquisition strategy for the big players. In particular, how successful are the big players going to be at nurturing young, startup, maybe even upstart brands? Also, what happens if fashion changes and today's trendy pop brand becomes tomorrow's fashion victim? Of course, the other factor here could be that the startups are working monopoly-in-a-box business models; they are in the business of being bought out. Once the deal has been done, they can either retire and chill out, or start building their next upstart monopoly-in-a-box offering.

The main challenge of the monopoly-in-a-box model is making the "box" attractive enough to the third party. This involves not merely getting the creative advantage offering right, but also securing all the various intellectual property components, which can be addressed by getting good advisers, and by reading the market correctly, which is the bigger challenge. Here, the greater market insight developed over time by large, well-established players can provide them with a significant edge over any small player. The main risk inherent in the monopoly-in-a-box business model is that an interested third party is not found and that a deal is therefore impossible. There may be a need to write off all expenses and the return may be negative.

THREE SUPPORTING TRENDS

Existing alongside the four business models are three broader, looser trends: garage sale, intellectual property marketplace, and open house. These provide respectively a stepping stone, an enabler, and a radical alternative to the four business models of virtual monopoly.

THE GARAGE SALE

Listen to this sales talk: "We do not intend to use our patent portfolio to prevent companies from using our technologies as long as they are willing to pay the license fees." This may sound like the sort of patter you would get from a technology entrepreneur who is hungry for income. But no, it is a recent quote from IBM's vice-president of intellectual property and licensing, Gerald Rosenthal.[7] So erase from your memory all those impressions of the impenetrable Big Blue fortress. The doors are open and the goodies are available if you're willing to dip into your wallet. The choice is pretty good too. IBM still leads the US patent filing stakes. In 1999, it was granted 2,756 patents, way ahead of nearest-placed competitor NEC of Japan.

There is a bigger trend here, of which IBM is at the vanguard. The "garage sale" is also opening doors at other large corporations such as Dow Chemical, Texas Instruments, Xerox, and Procter & Gamble. This is a step change in approach for these sorts of companies, which traditionally have kept the tightest grip possible on all their intellectual property whether they were using it or not.

A principal driver for the garage sale trend is IBM's well-documented success at turning the outlicensing of intellectual property into a $1 billion per year source of revenue, most of which is profit. Another driver, or perhaps fast-follower, is the increasing interest by the large consulting firms in this kind of activity. Arthur Andersen, PricewaterhouseCoopers, KPMG Peat Marwick, and others have established special units to assist large corporates with turning dormant intellectual property into capital or revenue. The practice has become known as intellectual asset management (IAM). A further boost was provided by the publication of *Rembrandts in the Attic*,[8] whose title neatly sums up what the trend is all about. Just imagine rummaging around the depths of dusty corporate intellectual property portfolios to look for the hidden gems. Even better, follow IBM's example and set up a publicly accessible website[9] that enables any third party to do their own rummaging and then make it widely known that the licensing is a possibility.

The emergence of the "garage sale" trend is in large part a consequence of historic *laissez-faire* management of intellectual property portfolios by the old fortress companies. It is, in essence, a creative way of dealing with an intellectual property inventory problem. In some ways it relates to the hub monopoly model, but there is not the same opportunity for capitalizing on increasing returns that may arise from the licensing of a defined, high-value hub technology. It also in other ways relates to the monopoly-in-a-box model, but the box is not that well targeted or packaged for sale and the potential for attractive returns must therefore be reduced. The challenge for companies that are starting to embrace the "garage sale" trend is to transition into one or both of the hub monopoly or monopoly-in-a-box models. Some of the early "garage salers" already appear to be starting to follow this route. It requires greater strategic insight and capability than merely putting up a "for sale" sign, but should result in enhanced returns. It may be that operation of the new business model is made the task of a specialist division or even outsourced.

THE INTELLECTUAL PROPERTY MARKETPLACE

The "garage sale" has largely been responsible for establishing new marketplaces for intellectual property, a major benefit. Where do you go if you want to buy a patent or get a license on a new registered design?

Twenty years ago this would have been a dumb question. But today, there is a diverse and vibrant marketplace for intellectual property. Here are some of the options becoming available:

◆ *Buy direct.* We have already heard about the "garage sale" organized by the big corporates. Next, why not try your local university? They are very likely to have a technology transfer office or some such operation. Some universities, such as Oxford, even have their own independent technology broker organizations. In Oxford's case this is Oxford Innovation Ltd, staffed by seasoned business executives. Interesting opportunities may already be on offer.

◆ *Engage an independent broker.* BTG plc is a well-known example of an intellectual property broker that acts as an intermediary between patent holders and commercial parties seeking patents to license.[10] An advantage of dealing with a broker such as this is that the patents on offer will to an extent have benefited from the intellectual property and technology expertise of the broker in question. Some brokers, and BTG is a prime example, are also prepared to invest in the development of promising intellectual property and even in the development of the technology itself.

◆ *Visit an online marketplace.* There are at least two online marketplaces for intellectual property. The first is operated by Yet2.com (www.yet2.com), which essentially offers an internet-based matchmaking service between those companies offering rights for license or sale and those interested in licensing or buying. Yet2.com has some sizeable clients, including BASF, Bayer, Procter & Gamble, Shell, and Siemens. The second online marketplace is the Patent & License Exchange (www.pl-x.com), which has more of an exchange-like structure and includes useful tools for the valuation of intellectual property assets.

◆ *DIY market making.* If you are looking for a technology partner, perhaps do a simple patent search on a web patent database such as The Delphion Intellectual Property Network,[11] started by IBM and a dream for the small technology company with an interest in patents. Find out who is patenting stuff of interest to you and consider making an approach. DIY market making is similar to how it used to be

20 years ago. The difference is the range of search tools available and their ease of access and, of course, the vastly greater amount of intellectual property in existence.

A marketplace is just that—a place to buy and sell—and all of the usual rules and cautions of the marketplace apply. Nevertheless, this intellectual property marketplace is an infrastructure that either didn't exist previously or, at least, wasn't as accessible. It is an infrastructure of opportunity, particularly for the entrepreneurial business.

THE OPEN HOUSE

The last trend arises out of the actions of various anti-intellectual property movements. The best-known example is provided by the Open Source Initiative, a network of independent software developers. Its development model involves the free licensing of base software source code to an informal network of programmers, who then freely chip in with improvements. Ownership of intellectual property rights in the code and any improvements to it does not appear to be an issue. The development space is open to all members of the development community. Much of the software that supports the internet appears to have been developed on this basis. The "open house" is much like the traditional university model of free exchange of knowledge among academic researchers. The model is also similar to special interest groups in internet space in which free exchange of knowledge can be informally established on a global basis.

The Open Source Initiative came into sharp commercial focus with the development of the Linux operating system, based on the earlier work of Linus Torvalds. Linux is commercially significant because it appears to be a viable threat to Microsoft's dominance of the operating system world. Companies positioned to exploit the benefits of Linux include Red Hat and VA Linux Systems. It is unclear how revenue generation operates within an "open house" model. Presumably, you become a consultant and offer systems implementation and support services. If the internet presents an example of an "open house," the challenge of finding effective methods of revenue generation has become increasingly apparent from the dotcom collapse.

A major threat to the "open house" way of doing things must be from competitors that do not choose to operate in the same way. Consider the race to map the human genome, where a collaborative, academic-style public project with a free, open licensing business model was beaten by Celera's hub monopoly business model. A special problem is also presented by the newly emerging business methods patents that the US Patent Office is starting to issue. Nonetheless, the "open house" exists as a viable alternative.

CAUGHT BETWEEN VIRTUAL MONOPOLY BUSINESS MODELS

Let me round off this brief tour of virtual monopoly business models by returning to a couple of the themes and questions identified earlier. Both relate to situations in which companies and industries are transitioning between business models or have the opportunity to do so.

BIG PHARMA AND THE BIG CLIFF

What model should the big pharmacautical companies adopt for revenue generation after patent expiry? One clear option is the value-added monopoly model. Post patent expiry, the drug is sold on the basis of well-protected value-added attributes, which can include brand advantage[12] and even packaging innovations. A good example is provided by Bayer's branded heart drug Adalat, which garnered record sales in the year 2000 despite going off patent[13] long ago. The branding model might also work well in an over-the-counter (OTC) environment. Indeed, many large pharmaceutical companies are starting to introduce OTC versions of their drugs post patent expiry as a way of continuing some sort of revenue stream. Pricing in the value-added monopoly world is, however, likely to be premium rather than super-premium.

The hub monopoly model might also have application to big pharma. A strongly protected, potential blockbuster drug could conceivably form the basis for a technology hub. The revenue-generation model then becomes licensing to any company that can meet the strict quality requirements of drug manufacture and distribution. Super-premium licensing terms may be difficult to achieve with a number of manufacturers and sellers in the market. However, post patent expiry revenue streams might therefore also fall off less rapidly. The "big cliff" will have been smoothed. There may even be opportunities to enter situations of increasing returns as different uses and users for the hub technology solutions are explored by the inevitably greater number of parties involved.

Adopting a hub monopoly model would radically alter the face of a big pharmaceutical company. It would change from being a highly integrated mammoth to a slim structure essentially comprising only a creative research (drug discovery) core, a closely integrated team of intellectual property advisers, and an outlicensing wing; some accountants may also be necessary to count the licensing revenues. Drug development technologists and regulatory advisers could be included within the organization, but more likely would form a standalone specialist company. The ongoing cost of integrated manufacturing, supply, distribution, and marketing organizations could certainly be jettisoned. Big pharma of the future could end up looking more like ARM. If this sounds far-fetched, don't forget that just ten years ago ARM, or rather Acorn, used to make and sell products. Now it only does business in intellectual property.

XEROX IN A WORLD OF COMPETITION

Xerox is still searching for a way beyond its Federal Trade Commission-enforced "big cliff" of 1975 that ended its absolute dominance in copiers. In the 1970s, Xerox's famous Palo Alto Research Center (Xerox PARC) established itself as a pioneering innovator of the personal computing industry. These innovations could have powered the company into new business areas, but instead resulted in a classic business school case study of missed opportunity.[14] The root of the problem seems to have been finding ways to exploit groundbreaking technology within an essentially copier-focused organization. Making things even worse, that organization had grown comfortable because it was cushioned by a fortress business space.

In recent years, Xerox has been successful at spinning out a number of technology companies building on Xerox PARC innovation. In the late 1990s it started experimenting with "garage sale" approaches to creating value from dormant intellectual property, much of which seems to originate from Xerox PARC. The "garage sale" was conducted under the direction of a new CEO, Rick Thoman, who joined the company from IBM.[15] All this, however, seems to tinker at the edges of the essential paradox that arises when the creative advantage from Xerox PARC meets the Xerox organization structure. Such tinkering probably also distracts from the main business focus. The first year of the new millennium was a disastrous one for Xerox in which its share price plummeted by 75 percent. Its market capitalization on January 1, 2001 was $3.1 billion, which equates to less than one fifth of annual revenues!

I have a radical suggestion: Keep the main Xerox business tightly focused on value-added monopoly model improvements to copiers, printers, documents, and other aspects of the traditional office space. Then set Xerox PARC[16] free as a separate company and let it explore hub monopoly, monopoly-in-a-box, and even open house models. The first two are powerful virtual monopoly models for creating value from technology advantage, neither of which fits with the traditional Xerox way of doing business. And if this all seems naïve, let me warn you that in the next chapter we are going to hear how a large, technology-rich but bureaucratically complex, loss-making conglomerate followed exactly that path. Its technology and intellectual property specialist arm is now a vibrant and fast-growing technology company.

SEPARATE OUT THE INTELLECTUAL PROPERTY RICHES

All the suggestions made above lead us toward company and organization structures that separate out intellectual property-rich parts from operational parts. The role of the intellectual property-rich parts becomes leveraging value from virtual monopoly business models. This applies equally well to slim and trim pharma as it would to an independent Xerox PARC. The intellectual property-rich parts can be established as separate independent companies, or they can be configured as focused entities within a larger corporate structure. In either case, they are appropriately termed intellectual property companies. The next chapter introduces some surprising examples of this sort of company.

4

THE INTELLECTUAL PROPERTY

COMPANY

HERE ARE COMPANIES THAT HAVE NOT ONLY MADE INTELLECTUAL property part of their business model, but have taken things much further. So much further, in fact, that intellectual property has become part of their mindset and their reason for existence. These are the "intellectual property companies" for which business models based on virtual monopoly are a way of life. As we will soon see, there are many more of them than might at first be imagined.

TWO MYTHS OF INTELLECTUAL PROPERTY

The chapter includes stories that at once dispel two major myths:

◆ *Myth 1: Focus on intellectual property is a "new economy" thing.* There was at least one company exploiting business models based on intellectual property way back in the nineteenth century. It is timely to revisit the story of that corporate pioneer whose approach established the trend for many intellectual property giants of the "old economy."
◆ *Myth 2: Intellectual property is only for big corporations.* We will meet a company that only started to generate real, major value from intellectual property once its big corporate baggage had been discarded.

Then we will meet an example of a one-person intellectual property company in the form of an exceptional individual who derives value from an intellectual property estate extending to 70 countries. Her business empire is managed from a home office in a leafy English village.

MISSION STATEMENT OF THE INTELLECTUAL PROPERTY COMPANY

Here is a novel form of mission statement, taken straight from a recent ARM annual report[1]:

> ARM is an intellectual property company whose assets are its people, patent portfolio, design methods and experience rather than physical assets. We are not involved in manufacture, but instead are focused on the creation of ideas and designs.

What is most interesting about ARM's mission statement is not its uniqueness, but that with slight amendment it could apply to almost any major "old economy" company. What ARM has done is to recognize the promise of intellectual property and allowed that to drive its business model. Here is that slightly amended version:

> Old Economy Products Inc. is an intellectual property company whose assets are its people, patent, and trade mark portfolio, business methods, and experience rather than physical assets. We are involved in manufacture, but are also focused on the creation of ideas for new and improved products.

This amended mission statement could well apply to any major consumer goods company such as Unilever, Colgate-Palmolive, or Gillette. These companies own an extensive and enviable portfolio of trade marks protecting their brand names and a similarly extensive portfolio of patents relating to product and process technologies. These portfolios establish virtual monopoly spaces around their brand and technology-differentiated products, which can then be sold at premium prices. The value of the companies is largely determined by the desirability, defensibility, and scope of those exclusive spaces. The amended mission statement could also apply to a large pharmaceutical company such as Pfizer, Merck, or GlaxoSmithKline. These companies are in the business of building strong virtual monopoly spaces around patented blockbuster drugs that deliver premium returns. Pharmaceutical company value is largely determined by the desirability, defensibility, and scope of the patented drug pipeline.

What I am suggesting is that the value of many large, established companies rests in their intellectual property. I am not alone in my view. A recent report[2] calculated the "intellectual property and intangible assets" values of a range of well-established companies as a percentage of total company value. Here are some sample numbers:

Johnson & Johnson	86%
Merck	82%
Nike	86%
Microsoft	95%

Those figures may appear surprising. However, start to ask yourself questions such as: How much would Johnson & Johnson be worth in the absence of its trade marks? Or, what would be the value of Merck minus its patents? The overall message is clear: Many big companies are already in large part intellectual property companies. This is so even if they have not got there by deliberate strategy. No wonder so many of them are now starting to think in terms of "garage sales" as a way of liberating more of that historically pentup intellectual property value.

MENLO PARK WAS IN NEW JERSEY

Before Menlo Park, Silicon Valley, there was Menlo Park near Newark, New Jersey. This was the location of the pioneering industrial laboratory facility established by Thomas Edison in 1876. The choice of location was deliberate. Menlo Park was out of town, with fresh air, fields, rivers for fishing trips, and above all lots of space and stimuli for creativity. The laboratory itself was well funded mainly through venture finance obtained by Edison and appears to have engendered an out-of-the-box "ideas factory" atmosphere—at one point the lab even kept a pet black bear. This was "Xerox PARC" 100 years earlier, only without the bean-bags. Its creative record was at least as impressive. The main achievement of Edison's Menlo Park was the creation of the electric lighting industry, as well, of course, as other fundamental inventions in the fields of telegraphy and the phonograph.

Menlo Park may have been an "ideas factory," but it was in no way isolated from industry and technical developments made elsewhere. It is clear from reading Paul Israel's masterly biography of Edison[3] that the absolute opposite of a "not invented here" culture pervaded the place. Emerging technologies from all over the US and beyond were brought in, tinkered with, rethought, and reshaped. Menlo Park was also in no way isolated from the world of commerce. The expected total output of the 80 research staff was "one minor invention every ten days and a major invention every six months."[4] Again, it is quite clear from Edison's biography that major meant major, with something capable of defining a whole new industry preferred.

The intellectual property imperative was equally strong. Everything with business potential was patented. Edison used the patents as a business tool to secure financing, to do licensing deals, and to establish new industries. Menlo Park's "product" was patents. This was an intellectual property factory, an intellectual property driver for Edison's business enterprises. A whole range of business models were used to extract value from the intellectual property created at Menlo Park. Many licensing deals were done, with often different terms and different licensees applied to foreign patent rights.

In September 1882, following a spectacular and famous public demonstration of electric lighting, the whole Menlo Park laboratory was moved to New York and became an integral part of the Edison Electric Light Company. With regard to the success of electric lighting, Edison is reported to have said, "I have accomplished all I promised." His other accomplishment was to apply the monopoly-in-a-box model spectacularly by providing the intellectual property rights and research knowhow on electric lighting to the Edison Electric Light Company. It received in one package the entire basis for a fortress monopoly in the technology of electric lighting and rapidly become a major player in US industry.

Edison is remembered as a great inventor. His biography removes any doubt that he was a pioneer in bringing research and development into the structure of the corporation. He was also a true pioneer of the intellectual property company. The Menlo Park intellectual property company used creativity as the driver, intellectual property as the currency, and diverse business models to liberate value. Each of these elements forms a common thread in our three stories.

NEMESIS AND REBIRTH

If Menlo Park, New Jersey was the birthplace of modern industrial research, the Central Research Laboratories of Thorn-EMI, located in Hayes, Middlesex, UK is surely where it reached its nemesis. In the mid-1990s Thorn-EMI was a sprawling, bureaucratic, barely profitable conglomerate engaging in disparate business areas, from making and selling fridges to renting televisions to licensing music. Its Central Research Laboratories had a long and prestigious research history dating back to 1920. Achievements ranged from early work on the development of radio and television to the invention of the CT scanner used for brain scanning. Many patents were filed on research output. Unfortunately, within the bureaucratic Thorn-EMI structure research output struggled to connect with business, let alone drive it. The research facility and associated intellectual property function formed a loss-making part of the conglomerate. Closure of the facility seemed inevitable.

Then in October 1996, a small team of managers proposed a management buyout of the research facility and the existing intellectual property portfolio. What would be the sale value of 75 years of research experience, 1,000 or so patents, and 500 or so trade marks? The answer at that time was $4.5 million, all privately financed by the MBO team. The new company, which called itself Scipher, adopted an innovative structure. The research facility would remain essentially intact as CRL, a distinct arm of the new company. The old patents and trade marks department would be reshaped as a separate intellectual property arm called QED. These two components could do business with each other to create new intellectual property, but QED's role would be very much to extract value from that intellectual property.

Within Scipher, the formation of technology spinouts would be encouraged, spawned by CRL technology and cemented by intellectual property created with the help of QED. Proactive transfer of technology into the Scipher group would also be fostered. For example, an outside startup company with technology strategically overlapping a CRL technology might be identified. An equity venture deal would be done based on both Scipher and the startup having a share of the equity. The company would additionally have the benefit of access to CRL's state-of-the-art research facilities and technology insight. QED would act as a freelance intellectual property broker and management consultant, possibly advising on licensing strategy or organizing "garage sales" for corporate clients. This would not only generate income but give QED a visible profile and contacts within selected client and industry groups.

Scipher's structure has two core components: research driver (CRL) and intellectual property value exploiter (QED). The overall framework is hugely flexible, with intellectual property forming the currency of exchange both between the cores and with spinout and equity ventures. In this sense it is very much like the flexible Edisonian structures that were stifled within the Thorn-EMI corporate bureaucracy. Scipher has stakes in a range of spinout companies, including Sensaura, a developer of 3D sound software, and MediaTag, which develops tags for preventing unauthorised use of copyright material. Equity ventures include Purple Voice, a specialist in voice over internet communications, and Silicon Display Inc., which makes displays for PCs. QED also helps the likes of Nortel Networks, IBM, Kenwood, and British Telecom with the management of their intellectual property.

Scipher plc was floated on the London Stock Exchange in 1998. Its market capitalization is around $1 billion. That represents more than a 20,000 percent capital return in four years on the initial MBO investment of $4.5 million. Scipher's success is built on great research, exploiting the value of intellectual property, and very flexible structures. It is also a business that operates many different intellectual property-enabled business models. It has a finger in many pies. Once again, Scipher itself makes no products—it is very much an intellectual property company.

THE ONE-PERSON INTELLECTUAL PROPERTY COMPANY

I met Mandy Haberman, inventor of the Anywayup leakproof child's drinking cup, at her home in a small, leafy village just outside London. As we sat at the dining room table, she told me the story of being a lone inventor with a great product idea and about the difficulties of raising finance or, indeed, interest from the established players.[5] She went on to tell me of a very successful product introduction followed by broad copying by infringers and the wide-ranging patent litigation in defense of her rights that followed. What interested me most about her story, however, was the end point, or perhaps I should say the current end point, since this is a story with some way to run.

Today, Mandy Haberman acts as the guardian and manager of the patents, designs, trade marks, and copyright portfolio that protect the Anywayup[6] cup in the 70 countries in which it is sold. She manages the various product licenses in each country and also the litigation against infringers, which has been similarly multinational. The product itself is made, distributed, and sold by others acting under license. In essence, Mandy Haberman comprises a one-person intellectual property company. How did she get to that position?

The story starts with her invention of the first genuinely leak-free child's drinking cup, a potential godsend for parents of toddlers everywhere. The invention was closely followed by the filing of an initial patent. The financing of international patent protection is quite a challenge for a sole inventor, so Mandy tried to interest some of the big players in the childcare market in partnering arrangements. None was willing to invest. One borrowed some product samples and didn't return them. Overall, the experience was disappointing. Mandy therefore decided to set up her own company, initially utilizing the services of a two-person startup product marketing venture, V&A Marketing, that was later to become the UK licensee. Prototypes and marketing materials were duly prepared and made public at a specialist trade fair. The response at the fair was incredible: £10,000 worth of advance orders were taken. These orders were fulfilled on the basis of the prototype design, thereby cutting any subsequent product development time down to zero.

At the end of the first year, the rapid success of the business was reported by the *Financial Times*. The article was read by the well-known designer Sebastian Conran, who offered to redesign the aesthetics of the cup to improve brand differentiation. This chance to add design value was seen by Mandy as important and so Sebastian Conran Associates were contracted. Very smartly, Mandy engaged them on a fee basis, which gave her ownership of all rights to the design output. At about this time, the trade mark ANYWAYUP was also registered. Gradually, a family of different intellectual property rights to protect different aspects of the product was being assembled. Intellectual property combination chemistry was at work.

The marketing chemistry was also working at full speed. Innovations included posting an Anywayup cup containing blackcurrant drink loose in a cardboard box to the buyer of a major UK supermarket chain. The box also contained a note saying, "If this reaches you without spilling give us a call!" There was no spill and a matter of weeks later the product was on the shelves of that supermarket. Within 18 months, the Anywayup cup had gained a 30 percent share of the relevant UK market. Foreign market opportunities were also opening up.

However, a black cloud came on to the horizon, in the form of infringing products. The infringers were large companies, at least some of which were those that had been approached in the early days and had shown no interest in partnering arrangements. Mandy bit the bullet and decided to litigate in the UK High Court, where the patent was held to be both valid and infringed. The defendant in that action appealed, but a settlement deal was eventually achieved. Unfortunately, the UK court case was only the start of the litigation, which has included actions in other European countries.

Annual sales of the Anywayup cup currently run at more than 10 million units worldwide. It was named a Millennium Product by the UK Design Council, one of a number of awards reflecting the product design achievement. These days, Mandy Haberman does not get directly involved in the operations side of things, preferring to work on new projects and to leave manufacturing and distribution aspects to her licensees. She still needs to get involved with the litigation, but the battle appears to be close to being won.

Mandy is a regular speaker at conferences for entrepreneurs. As a victim of infringement and a participant in litigation, she has directly experienced some of the negative aspects of intellectual property, but she is also a true pioneer of virtual monopoly. One of her great achievements is that she retains full ownership and control of all the intellectual property rights to the Anywayup cup. This was something that even Edison struggled to do with many of his inventions. Another achievement is her flexible but controlled approach to product development and commercial exploitation relationships. Mandy Haberman has shown that you can be a successful, multinational, one-person intellectual property company. You can also take on big corporate infringers if necessary, and win. And you can do it while working from home.

INTELLECTUAL PROPERTY COMPANY CHARACTERISTICS

These are stories of three very different types of intellectual property company. They can be added to the information about other companies such as ARM, Celera Genomics, and Powderject. What are the main characteristics binding these companies, in some ways very different, but in other ways very similar? There are three common characteristics:

◆ A robust, highly creative intellectual property generator
◆ One or more intellectual property value liberators
◆ Flexible organization and business models.

The third characteristic may be no more than a consequence of the first two, since one advantage of an intellectual property company is that it can be run on a very flexible basis.

THE INTELLECTUAL PROPERTY GENERATOR

The generator part combines creative advantage with expertise in intellectual property to build virtual monopoly positions capable of driving business. There can, of course, be different types of generator. There is the "auteur" model of the individual creative spirit, such as Thomas Edison or Mandy Haberman. This model is readily adapted to the classic creative team that comes together to create a new set of Disney cartoon characters or a Hollywood film. There can also be the industrial research model, such as that of Menlo Park, Celera, ARM, or CRL. Good generators combine excellence in creative advantage with access to the best and most creative legal advisers.

Close working between creatives and attorneys can assist in the intellectual property generation process. As Hugh Dawson, Vice-President, Pharmaceutical Patents at GlaxoSmithKline, comments:

> *"One of the things I really encourage amongst my team of patent attorneys is that they keep in very close contact with their 'clients' in the R&D organization. In that way, the patents side of things develops hand in hand with the research effort and we can ensure that smart patenting choices are made throughout the drug development process."*

THE INTELLECTUAL PROPERTY VALUE LIBERATOR

The value liberator can encompass diverse possibilities, but there are three principal types.

Architects
Architects create value exploitation architectures. Their expertise lies in matching the intellectual property generator to a business model architecture that maximizes the probability of financial returns. A clear example would be the architects behind the ARM business model, who

identified the hub monopoly business model as the way to exploit the intellectual property created by ARM's chip designers. Much of Scipher is about architecture. Indeed, redevelopment of the old, tired Thorn-EMI corporate structure into a defined but flexible architecture that enables both the creation and the exploitation of intellectual property is at the heart of the Scipher story. Architects need not be creatives as such, but they need a vision of how to establish structures capable of acting as intellectual property value liberators.

Hunter-gatherers

Hunter-gatherers create value-liberating relationships. For them, structure is less important than bringing together parties for mutual benefit and creating value-liberating relationships. The relationships can be relatively transient or longer term.

Edison is a prime example of a hunter-gatherer with great flexibility as to relationship options. Menlo Park was his supreme achievement as the pioneer industrial research establishment, but just six years after its birth Edison was content to merge it into the greater Edison Electric Light Company. That relationship shift was what was needed to create the electric lighting industry. For Scipher, hunting out relationship partners is part of its flexible structure: spinouts, equity ventures, consulting, or whatever, as long as it creates scope for real exploitable value.

Mandy Haberman is a different example of a hunter-gatherer. Her relationships are long term. For example, in presentations she still deliberately points to the contribution that Sebastian Conran made to the design of the Anywayup cup, even though that was some years ago. And as she told me:

> *"One of the reasons I litigated was that I felt an obligation to my initial manufacturing licensees, V&A Marketing. They helped me in the early days. In part, I owed it to them to go to the High Court."*

Brokers

Brokers enable buy–sell relationships. These are the people that create marketplaces. They may work in special units of the larger intellectual property-generating companies. They may specialize in one aspect of intellectual property, as does The Character Group, which deals in character merchandising for films such as *Star Wars* and *Chicken Run*. They may be online brokers like Yet2.com or the Patent & License Exchange. Or they may be companies such as QED, which acts as a broker for both intellectual property generated by CRL and for a number of independent clients. Brokers tend to act on a commission basis, but this may be worth it if they are saving you the hassle, and particularly if you can plug into their databases of likely customers.

FLEXIBLE ORGANIZATION AND BUSINESS MODELS

Each type of value liberator may be integrated with the intellectual property generator as a single company. The combination of the generator with hunter-gatherer and architect is, perhaps, the most usual structure for a fully integrated, R&D-driven industrial company. Alternatively, the generator and the liberator may be separate companies that come together to do business on an "as needed" and "to our mutual advantage" basis. Hybrid structures are possible.

One of the truly fascinating aspects of Scipher is that it combines a close, arm's-length relationship between CRL and QED with the possibility of "as needed" relationships with others. Scipher also comprises the architect, hunter-gatherer, and broker value liberators to give it supreme flexibility.

THE VIRTUAL MONOPOLY BUSINESS CONCEPT INCUBATOR

Almost all of the above discussion has been based on the premise that the intellectual property company is driven by creative advantage. This has traditionally been the case, be it electric lighting, consumer products, or a carpet-saving child's drinking cup. Creative advantage fuels the opportunity and the business model is adapted accordingly.

However, let us now flip this assumption on its head. The company could also be driven by the virtual monopoly business concept. For readers of Gary Hamel[7] this will not be such a wild proposal.

Imagine this scenario: The starting point for the business is the identification of a desirable virtual monopoly space, perhaps based on a novel application of an emerging technology. Let us say it is a space in which the emerging technology of wireless internet is applied in a new way to the supermarket sales environment. The intellectual property required to own that "wireless supermarket" space is developed in tandem with a framework for the virtual monopoly business concept, perhaps a technology hub or a monopoly-in-a-box concept. In this scenario, the virtual monopoly business concept drives the creative and legal effort. To make it really work, supermarket sales creative must meet technology visionary, patent attorney, and business model developer in a strange, but potentially explosive, symbiotic mix.

I know of and work with companies that are employing just such approaches. I am being asked to construct intellectual property portfolios that not just protect technology, but also define the virtual monopoly spaces in which those technologies will play out. I know of at least one patent attorney who has left a large, well-respected private practice to focus on becoming a "virtual monopoly business concept developer."

Good patent attorneys who are well used to spending time looking at technology patents are adept at identifying those potentially desirable, but not yet occupied, virtual monopoly spaces. As with all these apparently revolutionary suggestions, there is an example from history to prove that nothing is really that new: Xerox's virtual monopoly in "copier space" was originally developed by Chester Carlson, a patent attorney who invented the xerographic process, wrote the patent, and saw the market potential of its use as a commercial business concept.

PART TWO

CHALLENGES FOR THE VIRTUAL MONOPOLY BUILDER

5

ESTABLISHING SPACE WITHIN
THE CROWD

T HE INTELLECTUAL PROPERTY ENVIRONMENT PRESENTS AN IMMENSELY crowded canvas to the creative company. The numbers of patent and trade mark filings have escalated across the globe, and are at higher levels than ever before. New kinds of intellectual property are emerging, and with them new kinds of infringing situations. The risk of collision with holders of competing intellectual property rights, be they lightweights or heavy hitters, is also increasing. Developing products in this sort of environment can present a stimulating business challenge: establishing space to operate within the crowd.

SENSING THE MOOD ON THE FRONT LINE

In my day-to-day practice, I sense different effects and different moods in different parts of the company.

At executive board level, there is a sense that something new and different is in the air. There is an awareness of headline stories of multi-million-dollar intellectual property suits and of articles describing "patent wars."[1] A growing threat is sensed, but there is also an appreciation of the almost overwhelming complexity of it all. For many companies this is giving rise to simple "toolup" strategies that counter complexity with defensive investment in intellectual property, particularly in patents. As an executive board member of a very successful high-technology company recently told me:

"I'm not interested in the details of intellectual property or in starting any needless battles. But, if there is going to be a pissing match, then I certainly want us to have something to piss back in response. That is a principal reason that we file patents."

Bill Gates is reported to have advocated "patenting as much as we can," presumably for very similar reasons, following a tussle with IBM in the mid-1990s.[2]

On the project management front line, business and technology managers have become increasingly subject to intellectual property risk and the costs and delay that result from it. In one scenario from recent personal experience, an R&D director is running multiple technology projects side by side, well aware that all of them are subject to risk from third-party intellectual property rights. In another, a product design manager is beginning to dread the day that the weekly update of competitive patent and design publications becomes public and a further raft of potential problems is identified. In a further scenario, a production manager is seeing a carefully assembled relationship with a supplier disintegrate amid squabbles over how to handle a recently emerged third-party patent problem.

From discussions with colleagues, I know that similar situations are being repeated across broad areas of business and technology. At this level, the newly crowded environment has become an ongoing source of discomfort and frustration.

On the creative front line, there is enhanced awareness of intellectual property. Perhaps not surprisingly, that awareness is largely opportunity driven, with a focus on seeking to protect creative output. For many creatives it has, however, become frustrating as creative ambitions are thwarted by the existence of blocking third-party intellectual property. In a couple of recent experiences I have seen whole teams of technologists under a cloud of "creative block." They perceive all avenues to creative product development to be blocked by competitor patents. Finding a way forward seems impossible. In other instances I have seen creative people dragged unavoidably into the mire of intellectual property disputes, or spending a great deal of time establishing patents for purely defensive purposes. Some creatives are beginning to turn their back on intellectual property out of disillusionment.

The overall front-line picture is mixed, but increasingly unsatisfactory. At the executive level a complex threat is perceived and defensive actions are being taken, some of which can only serve to ramp up the overall situation. On the operational front line, the crowdedness and uncertainty are resulting in cost and delay. And for the grass roots creatives there are mixed experiences, some of which are leading to frustration with intellectual property as a whole. The real risk in the emerging situation may not be that of litigation and battles, but of creativity being killed off in the complexity of it all. This is too major a risk for any company to ignore.

THE STRATEGIC CHOICE FOR BUSINESS

The crowded canvas in large part reflects the creative and technology revolution that we are currently experiencing. It is a problem of creative success, and therefore in many ways should be embraced as positive. Nevertheless, since it is linked with intellectual property, which is a creature of legal monopoly and a gateway to litigation, it has the potential to become negative. It all comes down to how business chooses to handle it. There are essentially two choices:

◆ Business applies positive, thoughtful strategic approaches to dealing with the newly crowded environment, using intellectual property creatively and intelligently and the power of litigation selectively
◆ Business applies defensive/aggressive approaches that feed the negative aspects of the crowded canvas. A messy, litigation-driven scenario evolves, possibly involving abuses of virtual monopoly positions.

I firmly believe that business should make the first choice. However, new and different approaches are required. Steps can be taken at each of the strategic, operational, and creative levels, but the balance of action should be at the strategic and creative levels. This goes against the grain of traditional intellectual property risk management, which regards the risk as largely an operational matter.

FOUR STRATEGIES FOR BEATING THE CROWDS

The crowded canvas can be viewed through the lenses of four different field glasses. This leads to four very different strategic mindsets:

Field glasses	*Strategic mindset*
Project management issue	Fervent firefighter
Legal complexity issue	Earnest evaluator
Fight for space issue/opportunity	Dynamic dealer
Creative issue/opportunity	Confident creator

The first pair of strategic mindsets represents the more traditional ways of dealing with arising intellectual property risk as a potential issue. The second pair is evolving and views intellectual property risk as both a potential issue and an opportunity.

Fervent firefighters view third-party intellectual property risk as an operational matter. Assessments are made at a project management level along with the other numerous project risk factors, including market, regulatory, financial, and organizational. Typically, investigations are made toward the end of a product, service, or brand development project as part of a pre-commercialization clearance checklist.

This approach works reasonably well in an uncrowded intellectual property environment. However, in the new crowded canvas it can break down. The complex risk pattern is too wide-ranging to deal with as just another project issues box to be ticked. Many potential fires are probably burning and to fight or even consider all of them is likely to overburden the project management process, particularly if the fires are discovered at a late stage.

Earnest evaluators engage in early, diligent analysis of the legal risk posed by third-party intellectual property. They invest heavily in resources for research and early assessment of third-party intellectual property by their legal advisers. Careful decisions are made as to what to do with identified risks. Design-arounds will be considered, or even early licensing or acquisition deals. Occasional balanced risks will be taken where the identified third-party rights are believed to be indefensible.

These companies build up good knowledge of the overall competitive intellectual property landscape. They are therefore also more likely to identify companies that are infringing, or setting themselves up to infringe, their own intellectual property. The earnest evaluators may find themselves more frequent defenders of their own virtual monopoly spaces.

Dynamic dealers make little or no proactive assessment of competitive intellectual property. Risks become known to them as a result of third-party threats and/or direct legal action. Dynamic dealers keep on good terms with lawyers who are skilled at defending lawsuits or at brokering deals. They set aside fighting funds and have careful strategies for managing the potential PR consequences of disputes becoming public.

Dynamic dealer companies create intellectual property rights for defensive reasons, such as for use as bargaining chips to resolve disputes. They will not routinely monitor the market for infringements of their own intellectual property rights, but may scavenge for such infringements if threatened. They may also try to set up broad cross-licensing deals with strategic competitors, thereby removing sources of risk in a blanket fashion.

Confident creators view the crowded intellectual property environment as a creative challenge. They invest in resources for researching the third-party intellectual property environment. And, like the earnest evaluators, they build up a good knowledge of the overall competitive landscape. This is, however, merely a backdrop and a springboard to their creative aspirations. They start with spotting the available niches, the remaining uncrowded spaces, but niche activity is not their real goal. They are in the business of creating new space through clear, confident differentiation, which enables them to cut through or rise above the crowd.

ACHIEVING THE RIGHT STRATEGIC MIX

The confident creators have got it mostly right. They have identified the real challenge, the real opportunity of the crowded canvas. It is all about establishing big, bold creative advantage. This strategy should be the one given most weight by the company seeking to build the most desirable virtual monopoly spaces. Nevertheless, a healthy mix of strategies is appropriate for most companies, even those capable of confident creation.

The days of the fervent firefighter strategy are numbered, although this is the way that many companies still operate. These are the companies whose projects are increasingly sidelined by intellectual property issues. They need to change the point at which intellectual property risk is addressed, either hitting it early as the early evaluators do, or tightening their belts and dealing with it later as in the higher-risk dynamic dealer strategy. This is the key strategic choice for most companies. If this appears too bold and clean cut, that is deliberate. Anything woollier will simply place the problem back at the project management level, where it will continue to cost money in terms of delay and uncertainty.

Here are some pointers to help you decide.

EARNEST EVALUATOR STRATEGY

This is most applicable to companies that meet one or more of the following characteristics:

◆ Significant investment in creative development of products/services. The company has much to lose if an intellectual property dispute arises, or even worse if an injunction forcing withdrawal from the market is received.
◆ Narrow range of products/services. A dispute or injunction will therefore have a major effect on the company's product/service offering as a whole.
◆ Long market lifetime of products/services. A dispute may severely hamper market introduction and an injunction may require withdrawal from the market.

♦ Competitors prepared to litigate. The risk of being sued for intellectual property infringement is therefore greater.

♦ Outside venture capital required. These days venture capitalists are more aware of intellectual property. If you are seeking finance, be prepared for questions and even to indemnify investors against intellectual property risk.

The earnest evaluator strategy could, for example, fit well with a big pharma company making a major investment in new drug molecules; an internet portal provider offering only one specialist service; a major brand developer looking to develop brand value over a long market lifetime; any industry in which litigation occurs regularly; and a high-technology startup seeking venture capital finance. The strategy is not necessarily driven by the size of the company, although larger companies will be able to afford to spend more on evaluating risk.

DYNAMIC DEALER STRATEGY

This is most applicable to companies to which one or more of the following characteristics applies:

♦ Minor investment in developing creative products/services, therefore little is lost if a dispute arises. Rapid designing around is also probably not complex.

♦ Diverse range of products/services. A dispute arising in one part of the range may not significantly affect the company as a whole, even if market withdrawal of the product/service is the consequence.

♦ Fast-moving market, short market lifetime of products/services. Any intellectual property risk is therefore more transient, although in many countries injunctions can be obtained very quickly.

♦ Willingness to fight disputes. If the dynamic dealer company is prepared and willing to fight this can deter all but the most determined rights holder.

♦ Operating in a market where players are open to doing deals. Where there is a culture of doing deals to resolve disputes, this leads to intellectual property risk being dealt with as it arises.

◆ Fully financed. There is therefore no scrutiny of intellectual property factors by a potential financier.

The dynamic dealer strategy classically applies to industries involving poorly differentiated or wide-ranging markets for goods and services. However, it can also apply where the market opportunity is so fast moving that the company can not afford delay. Much of the IT industry probably fits into this category, and it is certainly an industry that has not been averse to patent disputes in recent years. The "dynamic dealer" strategy also applies if the industry as a whole tends to encourage deal making. It is often said that Asian culture can be more open to deal making than to conflict, which may make this strategy attractive where the large competitors are from countries such as Japan or Korea.

CONFIDENT CREATOR STRATEGY

The confident creator strategy should be part of the strategic mix of any company that intends to build a virtual monopoly. It provides a way to cut through, even to rise above, the crowd.

Cut through the crowd

You may remember an advertisement for Orange, a European telecommunications provider, which opens on a crowded Chinese city street. Many hundreds of bicycles and their riders move in slow motion in a single direction away from a grimy factory that pumps filth into the air. The colours are gray, green, and generally grim and the feel is unidimensional and claustrophobic. Then there is a glint of orange as we slowly perceive a lone cyclist with an orange flag riding confidently, cutting across the general, gray flow. The color and confidence of the rider strongly differentiate her from the background crowd. The advertisement ends with the slogan: "The future's bright, the future's Orange." The message of the advertisement is one of confident differentiation, creative difference, and a new direction that cuts cleanly across the grayness of the crowd.

I have seen many examples of the power of this kind of message applied in my day-to-day practice. The message applies when a trade mark client asks for a clearance search on a mark that immediately strikes you as different and clever. You do the search and nine times out of ten it is clear, and the opportunity is there to apply for broad protection.

The converse applies when the suggested mark immediately stands out as being descriptive, dull, or commonplace, such as "blue chip" for financial services or "smart systems" for computing. It is even worse when the search comes back showing a crowded picture of risk and the client still decides to go ahead and use the name. Five years down the road, they will be the ones with the weak, probably unregistrable mark. They will be the ones engaging in time-wasting, knockabout battles with other companies using other similarly weak marks.

The creative leaders do not play it like that. Brands such as Nokia, Pampers, Kodak, Marlboro, and Nike would stand out even if you had never heard of them before. They cut across the crowd.

In patents, the message is if anything more stark. All of my practice experience has shown me that the technology projects that get into messy, difficult, time-consuming third-party patent infringement problems are those that are just not that innovative. The way to get out of those sorts of problems is to admit that the technology is not particularly great, and to challenge the team to get more creative. Perhaps even take it further and use your company's propensity or otherwise to third-party patent problems as a metric of how truly creative it is versus the competition.

Rise above the crowd

Imagine yourself in the viewing gallery of the Empire State Building in New York. On the streets below, a million stories are unfolding and a million property holders compete for the available space. Now look up and embrace the soaring achievement of an architecture that rises above it all; a building constructed during depression times, but confident enough to play host to a big, hairy, aggressive gorilla. Taken to its limits, the confident creator strategy is not only a way to navigate the crowd—it is a way to rise above it.

I advise a team of medical device designers. In that technology area the patent landscape is hugely cluttered with incremental improvement patents from both big players and many small niche players. The technology team was at one point feeling increasingly under a cloud of patent-induced weariness. Their response was to get hypercreative, drawing inspiration from technologies outside their own direct spheres of experience. Over time, new and highly differentiated device concepts started to emerge. None of these was described in competitive patents and all of them are strongly patentable. Once the team was up and running in this direction, a veritable creative roll began. Great new concepts gave rise to spinoffs, which resulted in further opportunities. Confident creativity has enabled that team to rise above the crowd and to build new virtual monopoly spaces in which they (and not others) are free to play.

TOP TIPS FOR CONFIDENT CREATORS

◆ Make early surveying of the intellectual property landscape part of the creative process and not simply an activity done by the lawyers. Thus, for a technology project, define some general directions, get patent searches done, and build up a feel for the lie of the land. For a brand name creation project, similarly do some early searching on initial name concepts, e.g., to see if there are any companies already using similar names. The internet is becoming a fabulous resource for this sort of early surveying of the landscape. All of this is no different from a land property developer getting out and about and checking out new areas of town, new zip codes, and new opportunities for development. Spot the opportunities and identify competitive positions at an early stage.

◆ Extend the survey to look at other technology, design, or brand areas, not necessarily to spot risk factors, but rather to spot ideas to import from other areas of business. Creativity is not done in a vacuum. Use the crowded intellectual property canvas as a creative launch pad.

◆ Do not be afraid to change direction. If you do the above surveys you will identify third-party intellectual property problems at an early stage. This is good news, because the cost of dealing with such problems increases almost exponentially with the degree of lateness in discovering the problem. For example, if a search at the brand name creation stage uncovers a third-party registered trade mark in the name of a big, powerful competitor, then you can choose another name. The write-off cost, both emotional and financial, will be minimal at that early stage.

◆ Don't just design around. Use the need to change direction as a spur to creativity. "Design beyond" and "design different" are better ambitions for the truly confident creator.

THE NUMBERS GAME CAN DISTRACT FROM BUILDING VIRTUAL MONOPOLY

Many companies point with pride to the number of patents and trade marks they file as a measure of their creative prowess. Filing league tables are starting to creep into the business press. Some companies even measure the performance of their creatives and attorneys by reference to the numbers of filings made. There is a numbers game at work. However, far from being about creativity, it is largely being driven by defensive "toolup" filing strategies. There is a veritable intellectual property cold war involving many companies. The defensive activity certainly contributes to crowding the canvas, but it can also distract companies from being truly confident creators. Their goal should not be more filings, but more desirable virtual monopoly spaces based on bolder creative advantage.

As one example, consider the consumer products industry. Procter & Gamble is a company with a record of bold technology advances that it has used to form the bedrock for powerful brands. For example, Tide was the first synthetic laundry detergent when it entered the market in 1946. It is still a powerful brand today. Similarly, Crest was the first fluoride toothpaste and Pampers the first mass-produced disposable diaper. Both are still major brands.

In the late 1980s, the consumer products industry as a whole started filing many more patents. All the big players became involved in a veritable patents numbers game, an early example of "patent as much as we can" thinking. The majority of the patents were defensive on minor, incremental improvements in already crowded technology areas. Many patent attorneys were recruited. There was also a great deal of litigation.

The "nappy wars" consistute a rich source of case law for any student of patent law as result of the numerous tussles in the courts.

The general picture in consumer products appears to be much the same today. Procter & Gamble, Unilever, L'Oréal, and the other big players are still filing huge numbers of patents and disputes erupt at regular intervals. Nevertheless, cutting-edge product advances seem to be missing; "the first X, leading to power brand Y" is becoming a mantra from the past.[3] Could it be that the technologists are too focused on generating data to support all those patent filings to have time to be really creative? Has the industry drive toward more filings actually reduced the creative imperative? Is the numbers game distracting the consumer products industry from thinking bold and cutting edge? Is this pattern also being played out in your industry sector?

By way of a footnote, the Procter & Gamble annual report for 2000[4] proudly states that P&G applies for roughly 10 new patents a day, which is "well ahead of any other consumer products company."

ESTABLISHING BUSINESS MODELS WITHIN THE CROWD

Where there's a crowd, there's a platform to do business. The crowded canvas may present its own difficulties, but it is essentially an environment of creative players and one in which intellectual property has currency. There are undoubtedly new opportunities to be grabbed here.

Intriguingly, the opportunities may initially present themselves as risk factors or sources of frustration. Moving from surviving the environment to thriving in a new world of opportunity posing as risk requires a mindset that can turn a problem on its head and into a business opportunity. Why not, for example, view a company with an overlapping or blocking patent as a potential collaborator or potential acquisition target, rather than as a company that may sue you? Your biggest virtual monopoly business opportunities may yet arise from your biggest problems.

6

FIGHTING FOR SPACE

THE PREVIOUS CHAPTER DESCRIBED THE CHALLENGE OF ESTABLISHING space within the crowded intellectual property environment. That chapter explored how certain companies are "tooling up" as a blanket strategy to deal with the emerging complexity. Hints were given of a newly pervasive scent of aggression in the air.

The smoke signals are there and the lawyers have already picked up on them. In a recent poll,[1] 48 percent of US attorneys named intellectual property as the hottest practice area of the next ten years, knocking the socks off the nearest contender, corporate transactions, which gained a mere 15 percent of the votes. The business press has also picked up on the signals. "Patent Wars" was the headline of a recent article in *The Economist*[2] focusing on the growing volume of patents being filed and current patent battles. The advice given was: "Better get yourself armed. Everybody else is."

The language of war is also used in a recent book entitled *Owning the Future* and subtitled *Inside the Battles to Control the New Assets – Genes, Software, Databases, and Technological Know-how – that Make up the Lifeblood of the New Economy.*[3] *Red Herring*, a Silicon Valley journal of business and technology, has also picked up on the signals, naming intellectual property as No. 2 business trend for 2001.[4] The suit brought by the Recording Industry Association of America against Napster is one legal battle that *Red Herring* identifies as defining the spirit of things to come.

If we believe the signals, for many creative companies this first decade of the new millennium will be the decade not only of the crowded canvas but also of the intellectual property fight. It will be painful and it will be costly. The costs will be in terms of legal fees, damages, wasted time, and missed creative opportunities.

Does it have to be like this? Does more intellectual property have to mean more disputes and more litigation? Does the crowded canvas have to become a bloody canvas? I think that the answer is no, but that the signs are not good.

There is also an undoubted sense of courtroom battles bringing emotional excitement to an otherwise routine corporate landscape. What would you rather read about, the technology behind a new diaper, creating a diaper brand building on that technology advance, or the fact that the big corporate players in the world of diapers are scrapping it out in the courts again? This is not just a corporate preoccupation. The emotional factor can be a product of the court process. As I heard from Mandy Haberman, inventor of the Anywayup cup:

> "I enforced my patent in the UK High Court because I felt it was the right thing to do. It was expensive and involved a huge risk. I initially felt angry at having to take this step and was not at all looking forward to the court hearing. But on the day, I found myself caught up in the drama of it all. It was tense, anxious, emotionally draining."

FIGHT CLUB

To a crowded world of intellectual property ripe for aggression let us add some "fight clubs" with codified rules of membership, dress, and behavior, not to say elements of a totemic culture. These fight clubs of sorts are the civil courts, in which the players of the corporate world instruct their lawyers to do battle over their intellectual property claims. The rules of these courts, particularly in those countries following Anglo-Saxon legal traditions, are essentially combative. The parties engage in a legal "boxing match" and a judge, or in certain circumstances a jury, decides who wins and who loses.

Naturally, it is the fights that make it to the courts that are most often reported and discussed in the business press. These battles are public and therefore easily reported. Nevertheless, this is only a small part of the emerging big picture and perhaps not the most important part. It is in the world of privately fought disputes that much of the new risk and opportunity is emerging. Private forms of dispute resolution (e.g., arbitration) are becoming much more common. The fight scene may be about to go underground. Remind yourself of this next time you read a report of a big courtroom battle: You are only reading about the public face of the dispute, which may or may not be an accurate reflection of the true big picture.

Just as there may be different facets to a dispute, there may also be different sets of rules in operation. There are written rules, such as the various applicable intellectual property laws and procedures. There are also unwritten rules, such the one that says that the party with the deeper pockets (i.e., more financial muscle to keep a dispute running) is most likely to prevail. Differences in rule sets, procedures, and resultant costs between different forms of dispute resolution are often discussed in legal circles. For business, let me suggest that while discussion of these may be a concern, it is not the main concern. The big question for business is: What are we actually fighting for? This leads on to an inevitable subsidiary question: Can the courts really help us?

WHAT ARE WE FIGHTING FOR?

There are three main reasons for engaging in intellectual property disputes:

- *Recompense*—Gaining compensation for infringing intrusions into your virtual monopoly space, e.g., in the form of damages
- *Certainty*—Determining what the legal position actually is as it relates to a particular dispute situation or the industry big picture
- *Space*—Either expelling an intruder from your virtual monopoly space, or creating more space by seeking to invalidate competitive intellectual property.

To an extent, the courts can help with all of these things. Most media reporting tends to focus on recompense and major damages awards, but it is probably in the aspects of certainty and space that the courts can offer most assistance.

FIGHTING FOR CERTAINTY

In new areas of technology and business it is often difficult to establish where the exact legal boundaries are. The greater legal certainty that emerges from court decisions can be hugely important, not just for the immediate parties but in shaping industry practice as a whole.

By way of example, the fact that the area of biotechnology has been the subject of a great deal of patent litigation should come as no surprise. The new technology is giving rise to new legal questions and guidance is needed as to where the lines should be drawn. As another example, in the UK there has been much litigation relating to supermarket "lookalike" products that mimic the appearance of the brand leaders.[5] The legal question here is: When does mimicry become an infringing act? Again, lines need to be drawn.

A further example is Amazon's assertion of its "one click" internet business methods patent in the US against BarnesandNoble.com, a rival online bookseller.[6] Amazon was criticized for litigating by the press and particularly in the chat rooms of net space, but at least the judgments in that case will give us all a better idea of how these new types of patents should be interpreted.

The courts are good places to address questions of legal uncertainty, particularly in new areas of technology and business. In older, more-established areas, where the law is already well defined, the courts should have less of a role. Clear-cut cases should rarely need to be litigated, unless other factors come into play.

FIGHTING FOR SPACE

Sometimes a company needs a little help to expel an infringer from its virtual monopoly space. A court injunction against infringement can be a good way of achieving this. Many countries have developed summary or interim procedures to enable rapid, sometimes even pre-emptive, injunctions to be awarded against infringers. These procedures are perhaps most useful where the legal matter is relatively clear cut and the infringer is an opportunist risk taker. In these circumstances, negotiation is likely to be a fruitless exercise and speed of injunction is important.

It should be noted, however, that these procedures usually involve safeguards to protect the rights of the assumed infringers. If the matter goes to full trial and the injunction is found to have been awarded in error, damages may be awarded by way of compensation. In cases of strong virtual monopoly spaces and clear-cut infringing acts this is a minor risk factor.

Sometimes you are faced with a competitive intellectual property right blocking a space that you wish to occupy. For whatever reason, you believe that right to be invalid. Perhaps it is a patent that is not truly novel or inventive, or a trade mark that has not been used for more than five years. To be certain that you can occupy that space without fear of legal action, you may wish to have a court declare the right invalid. There are court procedures for doing this, but think tactically. If the right is truly invalid, an alternative strategy might be to ignore it. If you are sued you can then always confidently counterclaim for invalidity at that stage. And if the right is only partially invalid (e.g., claim 16 of the patent is novel and inventive), bringing the invalidity action now may only assist the rights owner to get its house in order (e.g., by amending the patent so that it is completely valid).

FIGHTING FOR RECOMPENSE

Major damages awards[7] often hit the headlines, such as Polaroid's award of just less than $1 billion from Kodak resulting from infringement of patents relating to instant photography. The ability of the courts in the US to award punitive triple damages in cases of flagrant infringement has also been well reported (something for which any potential "dynamic dealers" should watch out). Many court awards are not so spectacular, however, and the likely damages arising from winning a legal action need to be balanced against the costs involved in achieving the legal result. It is also necessary to factor in nonlegal and hidden costs (see below) and the terms that could have been achieved by negotiation. It is not unusual in complex intellectual property cases for the award of damages to amount to less than the cost of fighting the dispute. Despite the headlines, achieving recompense might be what the courts are least useful for in the case of many intellectual property disputes.

CAN THE COURTS REALLY HELP?

From the above discussion, the answer to this subsidiary question must be a resounding "Yes, no, maybe." On a practical note, there are three things that, on the whole, the courts struggle to deliver.

SPEED

Litigation can be a slow process. While interim procedures can move more rapidly, count on anything from nine months to two years to get a full trial decision in the US or the UK. In the civil law countries of continental Europe such as the Netherlands and Germany it may be slightly quicker. In Italy, it takes much, much longer.

Also consider the possibility of appeal. In major intellectual property cases, where the issues are complex or the sums of money at stake are large, there is often an appeal, which potentially doubles the timescale. As I heard from Mandy Haberman in the context of the Anywayup cup litigation, "When I won in the UK High Court I thought that was it, I'd won. But no, the decision was appealed. We had to start all over again." Better hope that your pockets are large enough to keep things funded long enough to get through the appeal proceedings.

GLOBAL CONSISTENCY

The rule sets in the courts of different countries are by no means uniform. Even in the larger developed countries, differences in legal rules and the culture of the courts can lead to extraordinary differences in procedures and costs. For example, in the civil law countries of continental Europe the procedures are inquisitorial and directed by the courts. In the Anglo-Saxon countries, primarily the US and the UK, the procedures are adversarial and the parties have greater flexibility in practical matters such as how much evidence to submit or how many witnesses to call. In many developing and, indeed, smaller developed countries, the ability of the system to deal with complex intellectual property cases at all is by no means certain. Choice of legal forum and choice of rule set can therefore affect the outcome.

COST

Litigation is well known to be an expensive business. A "ball park" estimate of costs for a straightforward patent case in a civil law country (e.g., Germany or the Netherlands) might be $50,000; in the UK it would probably be more like $250,000; and in the US $1,000,000. More complex cases may cost much more. You may get an award of legal costs if you win, but that is very unlikely to cover the full legal costs of litigating. There are also hidden costs and some hidden benefits that affect the litigant company.

HIDDEN BENEFITS AND COSTS OF FIGHTING

There is nothing like a nasty, prolonged dispute for getting intellectual property on to the organizational agenda. Almost instantly, awareness of the power of intellectual property is enhanced across the company. That awareness is a hidden benefit that can be channeled to positive effect.

As the dispute rolls on and skeletons start coming out of the closet (as they almost always do), there is an ideal opportunity to test the robustness of the company's systems for handling intellectual property. Even if the dispute is lost, the learning arising may provide a long-term source of organizational benefit. There are also hidden costs, however, and these can be very significant.

Distraction

Corporate energy will inevitably be directed toward the dispute and away from other things such as creativity, the customer, and bringing products and services to the market. Those directly involved in the dispute often find it a draining, even bruising process. Organizational distraction and draining are the most important hidden costs that need to be managed to avoid major impact.

A particular example of organizational draining is where all the best corporate attorneys are involved in long-running disputes. It is clear why they are selected for this task, but inevitably it takes them away from the task of building virtual monopoly spaces to protect the company's future. A further frequently seen example of distraction is where evidence is required to support litigation positions. Technologists get involved in generating data for patent litigation. Business managers are deposed and prepared diligently for their day in court as witnesses. Marketing people become involved in collating trade evidence to support trade mark cases. The dispute distracts all these individuals from their core task of creating business value.

Taking your eye off the ball

While you are battling it out with a known competitor, you run the risk of becoming blind to alternative competitive threats. Some unheard-of, upstart company may spot the opportunity to try to make you history in the market (the real battleground) just at the point when you think you are winning the fight. Turning this point on its head: If you see your major competitors battling it out in court, seize the moment and turn their distraction into your opportunity.

Corporate reputation

Public fights between major players hit the headlines. This may or may not be desirable. In one instance, a company may want to give the impression of being a tough player prepared to defend its rights. In another, it may prefer not to be seen as unduly aggressive. The tone of the media reporting will largely depend on how the battle shapes up. This is difficult to predict in intellectual property disputes, which are almost always of a complex nature. How this reporting will affect public and investor perception is even more difficult to predict. Corporate reputation should be considered when deciding whether to take a dispute public.

In a recent example, the UK High Court found one of Pfizer's Viagra-related patents invalid. The patent in question was not that on the

Viagra molecule itself, but a more broadly claimed patent relating to the PDE-5 receptor associated with erectile dysfunction. It is only the UK patent that is affected and the decision may well be appealed.[8] Nevertheless, it is easy to see public perception, even based on accurate reporting of the decision, shaping events into a picture that questions the robustness of the patent for the Viagra molecule itself. Those sorts of perceptions can affect share prices, if they are not very carefully managed from a public relations standpoint.[9] Given the choice, Pfizer might well have preferred to have this particular fight in private.

EXECUTIVE FIGHT STRATEGY

Intellectual property disputes have an impact on the company as a whole. In almost any company, the decision as to whether to litigate is made at board level. In many companies, while the decision is an executive one, it is made on a largely *ad hoc* basis. A more strategic decision framework is required.

My recommended approach is business model driven. Other alternatives are detailed below.

BUSINESS MODEL-DRIVEN APPROACH

We develop valuable virtual monopoly spaces and have at least some future expectation of having to defend those spaces from intruders. But we also have the confidence to consider other options, such as doing deals where the intrusion is not strategic. We expect to be approached in advance by any intruder. We will choose between public versus private arenas for dispute resolution and leverage any arising PR opportunities carefully to visibly signal responsible stewardship of our virtual monopoly spaces. We will even make use of the tools of "cultivate and reinvigorate" (see Chapter 9) to regularly review ongoing disputes on a portfolio basis. As a result of these reviews, we will prune out those disputes that distract and drain more energy from the organization than can be justified.

PRINCIPLE-DRIVEN APPROACH

We will respect the valid intellectual property rights of others and expect similar respect for our own rights. We will not hesitate to take action to defend our own rights if these are not shown respect.

This is the most commonly articulated big corporate strategy and it sounds great when you first read it. In practice, however, questions of validity and infringement of intellectual property rights are very often open to argument. This strategy has a great deal of built-in flexibility. Indeed, it is so flexible that its practical utility becomes debatable. On a cynical note, I have more than once heard battle-weary corporates suggest that "When it suits us..." should be prefixed to both sentences.

FINANCE-DRIVEN APPROACH

When faced with a threat of infringement action or a situation where we believe our rights to be infringed, we will do a cost/benefit analysis. If the numbers work out we will fight. If not, we will do a deal.

This is very much an "apply the formula" approach. The problem is that intellectual property disputes are rarely clear cut and even "ball park" estimates may be difficult to derive. Financial considerations must come in somewhere, but can and should they drive your strategy?

OPPORTUNITY-DRIVEN APPROACH

We will actively look for those companies that are infringing our intellectual property rights and seek compensation from them.

This one is becoming more fashionable, particularly with recent trends toward intellectual asset management (see Chapter 3) and using intellectual property as a direct source of revenue generation. This strategy can be an attractive option for large, old-economy companies with substantial underexploited portfolios of intellectual property. The risk, however, must be in the distraction that commencing such actions can bring to the company as a whole.

In one example British Telecom, the large UK-based telecommunications company, sued Prodigy, a US-based internet service provider, under its "hyperlinking" patent.[10] British Telecom has quite sensibly outsourced management of the suit to QED, a specialist intellectual property management firm.

KNOCKING OVER AUNT SALLY

An aspect of the evolving fight environment on which many commentators are focusing attention is the increasing number of invalid rights, particularly patents, that are supposedly being granted by Patent Offices. These "bad patents"[11] or "trash patents"[12] tend to be broadly claimed US patents in the areas of business methods and software. The US Patent Office has been under fire for poor examination of patents in these areas, and in June 2000 it even announced a "roundtable discussion" to identify ways of improving its examination procedures.[13] Its openness to suggestions for improvement is to be welcomed.

The "trash patents" froth has, however, been such that even the normally sober *Economist* magazine felt the need to wade in with a few paragraphs entitled "Patent Nonsense."[14] Specialist websites dedicated to addressing the problem have sprung up, including Bustpatents.com, which offers prior art searching services to help find prior art to invalidate problem patents. An even more intriguing service is that advertised by BountyQuest.com, which enables an interested party to place a cash bounty on the head of an identified "trash patent." The bounty is paid to the person who identifies the piece of prior art rendering the identified patent invalid. Jeff Bezos of Amazon is reputed to have backed this site.[15]

If we are to believe in the significance of all this, we could be in for a new sort of fighting frenzy centered on the "invalidity dispute." Nevertheless, in my view this is all knockabout Aunt Sally stuff: a problem set up to be knocked over. While it is certainly true that of the increasing number of patents and trade marks being granted at least a proportion will be invalid, this is no different from how it has always been. The court judgment of "infringed, but (partially) invalid" is nothing new. In fact, it is a rare patent infringement court case that does not put the validity of the granted patent at issue. When subjected to the in-depth scrutiny of the court, many patents are found to be invalid. The reason is that patent examination procedures are imperfect, or at least not as perfect as can be achieved in dedicated, highly expensive court proceedings. The focus should be on improving these imperfect examination procedures, rather than on whipping up new fights. There is a more serious problem that is very much worth fighting.

FIGHTING COUNTERFEITING

This chapter has deliberately focused on intellectual property disputes of a civil nature. In these disputes, there may well be fighting of sorts, but the parties are on the whole reasonable and it is largely a commercial dispute over products and markets. There is another sort of fight, that against counterfeiting. This is a different arena, where the protagonists are largely criminal and the ways of dealing with it reflect that. Enforcement methods involve private investigators, police raids, and potentially prison sentences for those found guilty.

The experience of counterfeiting in the developed world is usually a fake Rolex watch, Nike trainers, or Chanel perfume. It is hard to see any great harm in this, indeed it is easy to take some perverse pleasure in seeing the brand leaders being ripped off. Consider, however, living and working in an economy in which everything you buy is potentially fake. China is probably such an economy.[16] When I was last there many of the banknotes in circulation were fakes. The way to tell a good 50Rmb note from a bad one was to hold it in one hand, flick it, and listen for the characteristic cracking sound that showed genuineness.

Imagine yourself as a Shanghai taxi driver who buys a set of new brake pads. They may be genuine and reliable, or they may be fake and dangerous. You may not find out until you need to brake suddenly and discover the truth. Alternatively, imagine that you live in Xi'an and have Hepatitis B. You learn that an international drugs company has placed a new Hepatitis B drug on the market, but that despite its efforts counterfeits have appeared, which are high quality, at least in terms of packaging. You find a source of the drug, but do not know if it is genuine. If it is a counterfeit, you have no reliable way of testing what may be in it.

Then you hear that the drugs company has withdrawn its product from the market completely because it is unable to guarantee patient safety in the face of unstable, potentially contaminated counterfeit products.

These are not dilemmas that we have to face in the developed world where product integrity is generally assured. They should also not be dilemmas faced by those in emerging markets such as China. However, as a result of counterfeiting they have to be faced. This is a challenge for us all.

7

RELATIONSHIPS AND

INTELLECTUAL PROPERTY

INTELLECTUAL PROPERTY HAS BECOME A KEY CURRENCY OF COMMERCIAL relationships based on creative advantage. These include relationships with employees, with consultants, with development partners, with suppliers, with distributors, with investors, with licensees, and so on. These are all people you typically need to work closely with in order to bring a product or service to the market.

Create your own list of key relationships. The chances are that it is a list that has got longer because of broad business trends toward outsourcing, alliances, webs, development partnerships, and the like. Intellectual property will be there as a desired objective for the relationship, but also as a risk factor, a complication, and a potential flashpoint.

To set the scene, let's get on to the virtual couch and consider some examples of the challenges that can arise with the intellectual property aspects of relationships and try to identify themes and root causes. The chapter will then introduce some practical strategies for structuring effective third-party relationships that are more likely to yield significant virtual monopoly results with little space for disputes and wasted energy.

RELATIONSHIP CHALLENGES

You will have probably come across similar situations to some of the following:

- I paid a designer $1,000 to develop my company's new logo. It looks great, but he says that the copyright is his and he wants an ongoing royalty. He has sent me a copy of his standard terms and conditions, which I initially signed up to believing them to be a mere formality.
- Our global logo is a beacon for our billion-dollar business. As CEO, I've just received a letter from an old lady in Kansas who says that her deceased husband designed the logo 60 years ago for our founder. Her husband kept the copyright. His will transferred the copyright to her and suggested that she request royalties. The sum of $10 million is suggested. Their grandson is a New York lawyer.
- I don't like the style of our process-engineering consultant, but when I tried to sever her contract she asked for $100,000 in return for rights to the process knowhow developed to date. Haven't we paid for this already by way of her ongoing fees? What is the knowhow she's referring to anyway?
- I just tried to fire my UK chief chemist for laziness. He's a genius, but has done little work since creating that new dyestuff molecule for us. He reminded me that he owns a part share of the dyestuff patent, filed in his name. If I fire him he'll challenge the patent validity, ask for full assignment of the patent, and charge us royalties on our global sales of the dyestuff.
- We've worked for three years with Slippy Chips Ltd on a design for the SC3 microprocessor. It's a high-level, confidential project, which is close to market. Now I find out that Slippy has published a patent on the base technology, in its own name, without telling us. The patent is badly drafted; a shame, we could have written a better one if we'd worked on it together. Can they stop us selling SC3? That would be a nightmare scenario.
- We've just had an informal visit from Cosmetic Technology Consultants Inc. touting their new lipstick formulation that they want to license to us. It was OK, but way behind our inhouse

developed formulation that solves the problem of "shine texture." This is the main consumer concern, something we only found out through months of painstaking, expensive, and confidential consumer research. Imagine my horror when our new graduate recruit told them that we didn't like their product because it had poor "shine texture." I could almost see them licking their lips as they picked up that snippet of information. How long before we see their "shine texture" formulation on the market?

◆ Last month my firm invested $10 million in Web Plebs Inc. We loved its new business method, portal design, and rapid expansion plans. Today it received a writ for patent infringement. Its young management team claims not to have been aware of any potential patent problems when we signed the investment deal with them. Now we own 30 percent equity in a litigation issue.

DIAGNOSIS AND COMMON CHARACTERISTICS

All of the above examples are based on situations that I have seen over the last few years, with some artistic license thrown in. Common threads are:

◆ All are sticky situations. Some could blow up into bigger issues.
◆ All are potential time sinks. Some can be solved quickly, by paying up.
◆ Some involve commercial success and a desire to share in the rewards.
◆ Some involve "breakup" or "severance" scenarios.
◆ All involve competing claims, degrees of uncertainty, and legal complexity.
◆ All involve issues relating to ownership, freedom to use, or confidentiality.
◆ Different types of relationships are involved: friends; employees; consultants; development partners; commercial visitors.

You are probably now thinking two things. First, many of the problem situations could, in hindsight, have been avoided. Secondly, where is the contract, surely that would help to resolve things? Having foresight and getting an appropriate contract in place are both key factors in managing third-party relationships from an intellectual property standpoint. There are other factors at play, however, some subtle and others quite obvious.

ADDING STICKINESS

There is a need to take on board the potential "stickiness" of intellectual property problems in third-party relationships. Often, the "problem" is not the intellectual property aspect at all, but because intellectual property is a relatively complex area of law it can be used tactically to concoct sticky situations and leverage bigger issues. Getting to the bottom of it all can take time, and this time sink is in itself a risk factor for executives in a busy world. Paying up may seem to offer a quick solution, but think carefully about it and make sure that the payment deals with the whole problem.

As an example, I recently came across a situation where a client wanted to change his supplier of certain low-tech components. The supplier dubiously claimed design copyright in drawings of the components and asked for a once-off license fee of $40,000 in part settlement. The contractual situation between the parties was not entirely clear, and therefore the client decided to offer $40,000 to resolve the issue. What happened instead was that the supplier made a fresh demand for $800,000 for a full license, now believing that the design drawings had great value.

WHEN IT ALL GOES HORRIBLY WRONG OR HORRIBLY RIGHT

Intellectual property problems often arise when either there is strong commercial success, or the relationship ends and one party wants to prolong it or salvage some scraps from it. I often advise that you only need to think deeply about intellectual property if the relationship might go horribly right from a commercial standpoint, or horribly wrong and you will want to end it. However, most business people seek both commercial success and flexibility in creative relationships. This means that you almost always need to consider carefully the intellectual property aspects.

THE THREE HOT SPOTS

Situations of competing claims, degrees of uncertainty, and legal complexity are normal in intellectual property disputes in third-party relationships. The areas of contention are almost always of three general types: ownership, access, and confidentiality.

Ownership is usually the biggest hot spot. With ownership of intellectual property goes valuable rights, including the right to sell, to license, or indeed to sue for infringement.

The access hot spot comes about because one party desires access to any relevant (e.g., arising) intellectual property and the other party doesn't want to let them have it. For example, if you have a designer develop your product you may not mind if the designer owns the rights in the design, but you certainly want to be free to use the design in the products that you intend to sell. On the other hand, the designer might want to charge you a royalty for right of access.

The third hot spot, confidentiality, is self-evident as a potential flashpoint.

DIVERSE RELATIONSHIPS

The kinds of relationship that can become mired in intellectual property issues are more diverse than might initially be imagined. The examples from the virtual couch involved relationships with friends, employees, consultants, expert professionals, development partners, and investors. One example was of a historical relationship with an individual since deceased. The penultimate example involved an arm's-length commercial presentation, a situation of initial commercial flirtation, if you like.

EMOTIONAL FACTORS

This analysis has involved a rational, sober diagnosis of the given examples. In real-life, emotion and diverse motivations may drive matters in surprising directions. Indeed, if unchecked, emotion can become the principal driver. A minor issue can become a major embarrassment. The answer is not to get into these sorts of sticky situations.

THE NEW RELATIONSHIP FAD

There are many fads in relationships, and it seems right to embrace that tradition. Here's a new FAD to appease all those who have dared to suggest that intellectual property is dull. From my experience, making creative relationships involving intellectual property work involves three principal elements: foresight, agreement, and diligence (FAD). If any one of these is missing and the project goes horribly wrong, or indeed horribly right, then you will probably get into a wrangle over intellectual property. It is as simple as that. And this applies even if the reasons for it all going horribly wrong — or right — have little to do with intellectual property, just because of the natural stickiness and complexity of intellectual property issues.

The FAD factors can be applied to the broad range of relationship types; where they are least applicable is to informal or unplanned situations. Informal situations are best avoided from an intellectual property standpoint. Going back to one of the examples from the virtual couch, if you get a friend to design your logo on an informal basis, that favor may come back to haunt you, particularly if the logo leads to commercial success or if the friendship breaks down. Keeping things on a commercial basis right from the start is by far the better option.

One minor point is that the FAD factors are discussed below in terms of a party who wants to initiate a relationship. The opposite, potentially attractive but unplanned situation may apply if it is your company that is approached by a third party wanting to work with you. The FAD rules also apply to this situation. In particular, employ some foresight before responding in detail. Create some time and space for doing this. If the other side is worth getting involved with at all, it will respect your careful preparation.

FORESIGHT

Foresight means thinking ahead and asking some fundamental strategic questions. Asking these questions at the foresight stage is a low-risk exercise, because the relationship hasn't yet started and you are entirely in control of the process. The four principal elements of successful foresight are know why, research, scenario planning, and team resourcing.

KNOW WHY

Apply some strategic questioning focused on the fundamentals of:

◆ Why do we need to get into a relationship?
◆ How does it fit into the overall big picture?
◆ Do we need to do this at all?

To apply enhanced foresight, bring consideration of timing into the strategic questioning. That is to say, ask yourself when you need to bring the third party into the picture. If they are brought in at an early stage, they will have the opportunity to contribute more to the project, but they are also likely to want a bigger share of the spoils. Bring them in too late, and opportunities for joint creativity may be missed.

A good strategic compromise, using intellectual property as a control mechanism, involves taking the project to a point where at least the basic concepts and direction are established. Then put a stake in the ground, by applying for intellectual property protection for the base concepts. An approach to a potential third-party collaborator can then be made from a position of strength, because ownership of the base intellectual property is staked out.

RESEARCH

Good research at the foresight stage will avoid heartache later on. Research areas such as:

- Who might have what we are looking for?
- How can we attract their attention?
- What might they want from us?
- Will they be good to work with?

Enhance the research by seeking potential collaborators with a track record of creative advantage or with existing, useful intellectual property. Good research tools include the growing number of freely accessible patent databases on the internet; trade association resources, including those on the web; and general word-of-mouth sources of experience, particularly those within the company.

Make an assessment, however qualitative, of levels of intellectual property awareness, expertise, and useful assets. Also, research their intellectual property history. If there is a history of intellectual property disputes, this may be an indication that either they are very astute and aggressive or that they are difficult customers. Past history is often a good indicator of future behavior.

SCENARIO PLANNING

Introduce some elements of dynamics. Consider questions such as:

- How could this go horribly right?
- How could it go horribly wrong?
- How long should the relationship last?
- Where are the exit points?

Enhance the scenario planning by both plumbing the intellectual property depths of worst-case scenarios and ascending the heights of best-case success scenarios. Plumbing the depths perhaps encompasses some "due diligence," an umbrella term for making checks that all is as it should be, and that there are no hidden legal or financial pitfalls.

As an example, if you plan to work with a provider of gene database analysis tools in designing a new plant variety, double check that it has full ownership of those tools and, in particular, that there are no patent or copyright disputes in the offing. The worst-case scenario for this particular example is that there is a dispute, an injunction is served, and your project becomes "enjoined" by association. The best-case scenario is that the analysis leads to a plant variety that is a hugely profitable commercial success. This, however, may mean that the database provider comes knocking at the door for a share of those profits that have some link to success at the analysis stage. Plan for both best and worst scenarios, and raise any potential areas of concern at the stage of initiating the relationship.

TEAM RESOURCING

This is, perhaps, an obvious point. Consider the people side of things:

◆ Who from our side should initiate this?
◆ What support will they need?
◆ How will the relationship be managed?

To enhance the team resource assessment, think about the resources that the other party can bring to the relationship. Perhaps it has great attorneys, excellent information resources, or special business or technology insight. Turn this thinking on its head and also consider questions such as: If we work with this party are we going to risk giving them too much access to our existing team knowledge base? Never forget that knowledge flow is very difficult to control, and once lost it can be almost impossible to bring it back.

I see a growing number of technology consulting firms that as a point of business strategy try to develop contacts with a range of established industry leaders. Part of this strategy is legitimately to gain access to knowledge and insight developed by the leaders, through the "osmosis of insight." Over time, this gives them the potential to gain legitimate access to knowledge and insight greater than that of any of one of the leaders. A position of advantage is then established. Think about the Cosmetic Technology Consultants example from the virtual couch, where the visit from the technology consultants was entirely informal and the value-draining "osmosis of insight" happened unintentionally.

The four elements of foresight are all reasonably straightforward. What is key is that these are applied before the relationship is initiated. That is why it is called foresight. Also, be sure to make intellectual property part of the foresight thinking. That way you will not be like the man in the first example, who is surprised when intellectual property—copyright in his newly designed logo—unexpectedly raises its head.

AGREEMENT

You have applied foresight. It is time to take things further. You know why you want a third-party relationship, and you know who you want it to be with. You have thought through the scenarios and got your team lined up. You know what you are prepared to offer, and have a good idea what you hope the other party will accept. Now what you want to do is to approach the target. From an intellectual property standpoint, what you need to look for is agreement on at least five "must have" aspects:

◆ Confidentiality rules and rules restricting the use of disclosed information to agreed relationship boundaries.
◆ What is each party bringing to the table? In particular, what background intellectual property, if any, already exists for each party? If, for example, one party owns relevant patents or copyrights, this should be made clear from the outset.
◆ Who will own any intellectual property that arises from the relationship? A whole range of approaches can be adopted, from total ownership by one party to fully shared ownership, to more complex divides reflecting any differences in the parties' commercial priorities. What is important is that it is clear who owns what.
◆ Who has right of access to ("freedom to use") the relevant intellectual property? Agreements restricting use to certain commercial fields or excluding use from certain fields may be considered.
◆ What happens when the relationship ends? Continuing obligations, such as those relating to confidentiality, may be appropriate, even after the relationship ends.

PUT IT IN WRITING

I strongly recommend that once agreement has been reached, it be sealed by way of a formal written contract. In practice, what this usually means is that the party who does more of this sort of thing brings out its (or its lawyers') "house contract" and this is adapted to fit the situation. There will generally be discussion of the details, but this is no different from any other commercial negotiation.

Beware the standard contract that, for example, a design or technology consulting firm may ask you to sign. Look very carefully at the standard terms, which are likely to be highly favorable to the purveyor of the contract. If you do not want to agree to them, negotiate better terms before signing. In this way, you will avoid the situation where the consulting firm relies on its standard contract to assert ownership of the intellectual property arising from its creative efforts, even where those efforts are being paid for by a client who naturally, but naïvely, expects to own the rights to the output.

CHECK ALIGNMENT BETWEEN WRITTEN AND UNWRITTEN AGREEMENT

Whilst getting a formal, written Agreement (capital A) in place is always advisable, this will only truly make the relationship work if it matches the unwritten agreement (small *a*) between the parties. Many disputes arise where there is an imbalance or, indeed, conflict between the agreement as it exists in the minds of the participants and the formal contractual Agreement. Particular difficulties occur where there are personnel changes and new team members work against their perception of the agreement, which in fact differs in substance from the formal written Agreement. That conflict between perceived agreement and formal Agreement may only come out in the "horribly right, horribly wrong" scenario. Don't get burnt. When new team members become involved, make absolutely sure that they understand what the relationship and the Agreement are really about.

Balance

Good agreements between commercial parties represent a balance. This involves different elements, including balance of power; balance of access to capital; balance of influence; and balance of creativity. It goes without saying that as commercial relationships develop, the balance can shift.

Good Agreements fairly reflect that balance. Bad Agreements are unbalanced, and these are the ones that are likely to give rise to disputes, particularly where a shift pushes the imbalance into the realms of the unacceptable. From experience, those companies that make creative relationships involving intellectual property work effectively are both comfortable with the concept of balance, and set up simple frameworks to reflect that balance and any shifts in it.

Set up simple agreement frameworks

Set up standard types of formal Agreement with well-understood company guidelines as to when each type is to be used. One company guideline could be that before approaching any potential third-party developer, a confidentiality Agreement is set up with that developer. Where that developer can offer creative potential and experience, but has no existing intellectual property or capital to invest, a consultancy Agreement may be a good way forward. Under typical terms, the consultant receives payment for all work done and full ownership of arising intellectual property lies with the company. Where, however, that developer has some existing intellectual property and/or is willing to part fund investment in further creative activity, a development Agreement is probably more suitable. Typically, this includes apportioning a share of intellectual property arising. In each of these cases, the framework Agreement fits the balance of the relationship and the commercial interests of the parties.

A final story puts agreement into some sort of practical, business context. I recently advised a small high-technology consulting firm. It was looking to work as a specialist developer to one of the big players in its field, a leading multinational. I was asked to review the intellectual property terms of that big player's house development Agreement. The Agreement was some 30 pages long and immensely complex, but all of the right things, including the five "must have" aspects, were there. I reached the second appendix, which should have included a definition of the technology subject matter of the development project. This definition had been extensively referred to in the preceding detailed terms of the Agreement. However, the second appendix was a blank page.

When I quizzed my client, its response was that in its field the technology moves so fast that, although the relationship was due to start within a month, the subject matter of the technology project had not yet been defined. Both parties were, however, working on the basis that getting the legal Agreement in place could take a very long time. The pragmatic plan of attack was therefore to set up the Agreement first and then agree (small *a*) what the project would actually consist of.

DILIGENCE

Diligence is a term that is commonly used in the legal context of "due diligence." Here the term is used in its more general sense to mean the diligence (i.e., care and attention) required to maintain an ongoing focus on intellectual property once the relationship is up and running. There are three key aspects:

◆ Keep "know why" and intellectual property on the agenda of the relationship. For major projects, make it something that is reviewed by your team and by the parties jointly at regular intervals.
◆ Monitor any shifts in the balance of the relationship. If the balance shifts over time, the terms of the Agreement might need to be adjusted, renegotiated, or even terminated.
◆ Keep good meeting notes and establish ground rules for how to handle arising intellectual property matters. Adopting this approach will help avoid the sort of situation found in the Slippy Chips Ltd problem, where one party filed a patent without even telling its development partner.

To take diligence a step further, consider any creative relationships that your company or your team currently engages in with a third party. For each relationship, think about the creative output using intellectual property generated as a measure. Then think about the terms of existing Agreements, focusing on the intellectual property terms since these relate directly to the creative advantage expected to result. From this analysis, build up a picture of how effective each relationship is and whether the balance of Agreement terms fits with the current reality of the relationship. Apply cold, commercial judgment in making the analysis. Build up both a picture of the state of each relationship, and an overview of the portfolio of relationships. Then prepare to apply the tool of "cultivate and reinvigorate" (see Chapter 9) to the relationship portfolio.

What I am advocating is a high-level review process best carried out by someone without political or emotional attachment to any one particular relationship, possibly a senior manager or independent analyst. Indeed, it is the sort of review process that senior management will be well used to applying to project and business portfolios. The only difference here is the use of intellectual property output as part of the measurement criteria. Resulting action steps can include shifting emphasis or funding to the better-performing relationships, renegotiating terms, or ending the least effective relationships.

If the basic FAD approach has been applied, this sort of cultivate and reinvigorate process should not be hampered by any intellectual property stickiness or disputes. FAD is designed to build in the flexibility for this kind of portfolio review right from the start.

ADDRESSING THE RELATIONSHIP CHALLENGES

Below are some thoughts on how to address the problems from the virtual couch at the start of the chapter. Real-life outcomes will depend on multiple factors, including emotional factors and the ultimate motivations of the parties. The FAD factors (foresight, agreement, diligence) that would reduce the chances of these sorts of problems arising are indicated in brackets.

◆ $1,000 was paid to a designer to develop a new corporate logo. This is what the designer has done and the logo looks great. Now the designer is asserting copyright in the logo design. He wants an on-going royalty. This is not such an unusual situation. Ask to see a copy of the designer's terms and conditions on the basis of which the design work was done. These should define ownership of copyright, probably tucked away somewhere in the small print and almost certainly in terms favorable to the designer. Pragmatic resolution might involve offering the designer a small sum to assign over the copyright. An ongoing royalty is undesirable, since it is an open-ended commitment over the long lifetime of a copyright work. The overall message is more straightforward: Read the standard terms and conditions before proceeding. (FA)

◆ The next problem is the stuff of a CEO's nightmare. That global logo is probably one of the billion-dollar company's most valuable assets. The old lady in Kansas may have got it wrong, but there is a chance that her deceased husband did design the logo 60 years ago for the company's founder. The copyright may never have been assigned to the company and the will may have resulted in a legal transfer of the copyright. The sum of $10 million sounds a lot, particularly since there might be a legal argument that by not asking for royalties earlier an implied license to use the copyright has been established. The fact that their grandson is a New York lawyer is probably less important than the fact that she is an old lady, recently widowed. If she sues the company, just think of the PR consequences: Plucky Kansas widow takes on corporate giant over copyright infringement. Arrange a meeting. Aim to resolve this quietly and permanently. (FA)

◆ The process engineering consultant is asking for $100,000 in return for rights to the process knowhow developed under contract. Get a copy of her contract. The standard terms for a consulting Agreement should define ownership of all intellectual property rights to rest with the party engaging the consultant. Assuming this to be the case, go ahead and sever the contract. As a backstop, also ask the consultant to formally identify and assign ownership of all knowhow developed to date in accordance with the contractual terms. Remind the consultant of any ongoing obligations, e.g., confidentiality, that extend beyond the severance of the contract. (FAD)

◆ Your UK chief chemist may be a genius, but he has done little work since creating that new dyestuff molecule. Why not? This sounds like a management problem, and the patent and all the assertions relating to it are merely being used to add stickiness to the situation. His employment contract should make clear who owns the rights in the patent. Get advice on the details of his legal assertions, think about whether this is a relationship that can be salvaged or not, and plan a further meeting with him. (AD)

◆ A three-year-old, high-level, and confidential relationship with Slippy Chips Ltd has resulted in a marketable design for the SC3 microprocessor. The relationship appears to have been successful in generating creative advantage. A badly drafted patent on the base technology has unexpectedly been published in Slippy Chips' name. This is a situation where care and ongoing diligence appear to have broken down, since the patent was filed without prior notice. In any case, why had the parties not thought to file a patent jointly? Gather together all facts relating to the patent. Then carefully check the formal agreement with Slippy Chips, which should be a development Agreement including terms relating to ownership of arising intellectual property and freedom to use rights needed to bring the SC3 microprocessor on to the market. Get all the ducks in a row and then raise the issue. Overall, this is a situation where it is difficult to tell what is going on until it has been discussed. Possibly, Slippy Chips has merely acted naïvely. Not inconceivably, the patent may have been filed by another part of the company that was unaware of the confidential SC3 project. Possibly, it intends to use the patent for tactical leverage. If the latter applies, a good development Agreement drafted with foresight should include terms that will put a brake on Slippy Chips' tactical plans. (FAD)

◆ Months of painstaking and expensive consumer research have resulted in unique knowledge and insight into the lipstick consumer. You alone know that consumer's principal concern is "shine texture." That understanding is confidential to you and immensely valuable in preparing a consumer-relevant formulation for market. In hindsight, all members of your team should have been clearly reminded of that fact prior to the visit of Cosmetic Technology Consultants. They may be touting their new lipstick formulation, but they are also on the sniff for insider insight. They got it, courtesy of the hapless new graduate recruit who was probably unaware of the value of the knowledge relating to "shine texture." Expect a call from Cosmetic Technology Consultants in about six months' time wanting to sell their new "shine texture" formulation to you. (FD)

◆ $10 million has been invested in Web Plebs Inc. based on its new business method, portal design, and rapid expansion plans. It has received a writ for patent infringement. It is to be hoped that the pre-investment "due diligence" will have included some appraisal of third-party intellectual property infringement risk. On the other hand, it may not have. The learning here is clearly to do with foresight. If the patent litigation goes against Web Plebs, the consequences could be a permanent injunction and damages. That 30 percent equity stake could be worth nothing if the company can no longer trade. Get on the phone to a good lawyer. (F)

8

PUBLIC UNEASE

THERE IS A NEW CHALLENGE EMERGING FOR THE BUILDERS OF VIRTUAL monopoly, which requires thought and considered action before it becomes a significant threat. This book describes the benefits of using intellectual property as a tool for business. However, for a growing number of people the role that intellectual property plays in the economy has become a matter for serious concern. These people will have read much of this book with an increasing sense of unease, possibly even disgust. Their diverse concerns are increasingly getting media airtime and occasionally spilling out on to the streets in the form of public demonstrations.[1]

The challenge for the builders of virtual monopoly is to understand and respond appropriately to public unease, some of which is justified and some of which is not. Businesses can create areas of opportunity by responding creatively to the arising concerns. This is a challenge of positive, constructive engagement.

STRANDS OF CONCERN

There are two separate strands of concern. First, there are those who are concerned by the effects of global capitalism and market economics *per se*.[2] This book cannot respond to their concerns in detail. Virtual monopoly is undoubtedly a creature of the market. It does, however, give rise to new opportunities to transcend the traditional economics of capital, because in virtual monopoly economics creative ability is more important than access to capital. This can be a new and potent source of power for creative smaller players to take on the traditional fortresses of old-style capitalism.

Secondly, there are those who are concerned with the detailed role of intellectual property in the economy. Particular, often-voiced concerns include the following:

◆ Concentration of intellectual property in the hands of fewer, global players
◆ Use of intellectual property to establish abusive monopoly positions
◆ Effects on local economies
◆ Effects on emerging economies
◆ Patenting of the human genome.

All of these issues are worthy of public debate. The next few sections offer some thoughts on these issues, while appreciating the complexity, politics, and emotion behind some of them. The chapter then returns to the big picture and sets out why all of this has importance for business.

CONCENTRATION OF GLOBAL INTELLECTUAL PROPERTY

The economy has become more global. The scope for applying intellectual property at a global level has also grown. However, does this translate into a scenario where a small number of large, global businesses control increasing swathes of exclusive, virtual monopoly space to the detriment of the public good? If that were the scenario it would be worrying, but there are some strong counter-trends that should ease public concern.

The first counter-trend is business model driven. A strong example is provided by the "garage sale" in which the old fortress companies are opening up their intellectual property estates for licensing. There are still license fees to be paid, but this is a trend of access rather than one of exclusion. By way of another example, the hub monopoly model depends on adoption of the hub by large numbers of licensees for returns to be generated. Again, the trend is one of access to virtual monopoly space. In addition, the "open house" model advanced by the Open Source movement as a new business model to challenge the "hub giants" of the IT industry is just that, an open model of access to non-exclusive space. In many aspects, business model trends are moving away from exclusion.

The second counter-trend, one that this book seeks to encourage, is that smaller companies and individuals are increasingly starting to build their own, virtual monopoly niches. It used to be that patents and trade marks were the playground of the big corporations and occasional mad inventors, but this is no longer the case. About 25 percent of patents filed today in the US are from small and medium-sized companies. Similar trends are repeated elsewhere across the globe. And intellectual property is becoming the way that these small companies engage with the larger, well-established players.

In biotechnology the prevalent business track is that in which a niche player discovers a new advance, patents it, and uses the patent to gain funding and attract big pharma development partners. This can also be seen in the increasing number of companies that are adopting the monopoly-in-a-box model. Think about the smaller players that Cisco has bought out in recent years, often on the back of that smaller player's patented niche technology. This is all part of a bigger picture. Charles Handy describes a world in which large, corporate "elephants" engage symbiotically with small, niche player "fleas."[3] Increasingly, intellectual property is the currency and moderator for that elephant–flea engagement.

In summary, there is more to the growth of intellectual property than global giants dominating the virtual monopoly landscape. In many ways, there is a new paradox in which more intellectual property may in fact mean less exclusion, more access, and different kinds of big player–small player engagement. The mix is headier, but not necessarily more concentrated.

WHEN VIRTUAL MONOPOLY BECOMES REAL MONOPOLY

Virtual monopoly is all about legal monopoly rights in the form of intellectual property granted by the state to business to protect creative advantage. These can have real, positive value for business and for society. There is, however, another side to monopoly, where a line is crossed between the positive use of legal monopoly and the adoption of illegal monopolistic behaviors. I am talking about activities such as:

◆ Predatory pricing
◆ Cartels and collusion
◆ Excessive control of the market
◆ Abuse of dominant position.

These behaviors are illegal in most countries because they breach competition or antitrust laws safeguarding fair and open market competition. They also enrage consumers whose interests they adversely affect. The relevance to builders of virtual monopoly is that just as pricing and certain forms of collusive agreement can breach antitrust, so can abusive behaviors involving intellectual property. One challenge for business based on virtual monopoly therefore becomes to develop awareness of antitrust and consumer concerns, and to keep on the right side of the line.

The ongoing Microsoft case in the US Supreme Court has brought the issue of antitrust to the attention of the business community and the public at large. Microsoft is one of the true creative pioneers of intellectual property. This is one of its real strengths and a key contributor to its success. In part, the Supreme Court case is, however, concerned with the extent to which that intellectual property has been used to control the market. The eventual outcome of the case is likely to have industry-wide consequences.

Major brand owners like to be able to control how their products are distributed and sold. They want to ensure that the products are only encountered in environments that fit with the quality expected of their products. It is possible to imagine the owner of a jeans brand objecting to its branded jeans, sourced as parallel imports from a low-cost country, being sold at cut price in a supermarket. Of course, the supermarket owner will plead that all it is trying to do is offer its customers cheaper jeans. At the time of writing, the case of jeans manufacturer Levi Strauss vs. Tesco, a major UK supermarket, is receiving its first reading in the European Court of Justice. This case is about a subtly different aspect of the balance between open market competition and the rights of the intellectual property owner. It concerns the extent to which trade mark rights become "exhausted" by onward parallel sale and are therefore no longer available to the brand owner for use as a control mechanism.

EFFECT OF INTELLECTUAL PROPERTY ON LOCAL ECONOMIES

There are growing concerns that large, intellectual property-rich companies are using their virtual monopoly power to suppress local industry and business, whether it is your local café, garage on the corner, or a peddler on the streets of Mumbai. This is a fair concern. It does happen. Trade mark actions are one example.

My local newspaper reported the story of a local café that recently changed its name and invested in new signage, menus, etc. Within a month of the changes it received a letter from lawyers representing a medium-sized chain of restaurants that owns the registered trade mark for the café's chosen name. The letter bluntly demanded that the local business owners cease and desist use of the name of its restaurant within seven days or face action for infringement of a registered trade mark. The restaurant owners did change the name, but were outraged enough about their experience to contact the local newspaper. That article "named and shamed" the trade mark owner, which is now not very popular in our local community

In a second example, a one-man business represented by an accountant registered a new limited company name. Within a week, a similarly blunt cease and desist letter was received from a large insurance company demanding that the company name be changed. In that case, I advised the small company to make the name change but also to ask the insurance company for a contribution toward the cost of registering a new company name and printing new business cards. To its credit, the large insurance firm agreed to this.

Concerns about big business behaving aggressively toward small, local firms with intellectual property claims are therefore valid. And as intellectual property portfolios become more global, this kind of behavior is likely to become more widespread, possibly spreading to developing countries. However, consider these situations from the point of view of the trade mark owner. Its trade mark is one of its most valuable corporate assets. Of course, it is going to want to monitor for infringements, however small scale they are. If it does not do this, the value of its mark will become diminished by unauthorised use. Almost all of the major brand owners engage attorneys merely to monitor for trade mark infringements. These attorneys routinely send out cease and desist letters and sometimes take further action if the right response is not received.

The challenge here for the major brand owners is in the way that they engage with the small-scale, local assumed infringer. In many cases, the act of infringement arises only as a result of ignorance or naïvety with regard to trade mark law. In the second example I gave, the insurance company's action was reasonably fair. But why could their initial letter not have included some brief explanation as to what trade marks are all about and why the large company needs to take action to protect its mark? Or why could it not have proactively offered a small contribution to renaming costs? That would seem to be both good stewardship of its virtual monopoly estate and good public relations. Remember that contacting the newspapers to tell your story is always an option for the smaller business that feels unfairly treated. Big companies should use their virtual monopoly muscle with care and creativity.

EFFECT OF INTELLECTUAL PROPERTY ON EMERGING ECONOMIES

The effect of intellectual property in emerging economies, particularly developing countries, is an often-voiced concern. There are three main areas for concern:

◆ Misappropriation of local knowledge by global companies
◆ Lack of investment by global companies in local knowledge
◆ Use of intellectual property to deny local technology access.

The issues are diverse. The challenge for those engaged in building virtual monopoly on a global scale is to develop awareness of and sensitivity toward the issues involved.

MISAPPROPRIATION OF KNOWLEDGE

Imagine that a foreign company researches your developing country to gain understanding of your local knowledge and then tries to patent it. One reported example was US Patent No. 5,401,504, granted to University of Mississippi Medical Center for the therapeutic use of turmeric.[4] The use of turmeric as a traditional remedy in parts of India was known, as the patent itself acknowledged. How could a patent be granted on a known medical method? This comes down to a nuance of US patent law. The US is one of the very few countries that does not consider earlier use of an invention as prior disclosure unless it is "known or used by others in this country" (i.e., in the US). In most other countries, the prior disclosure by local use in India would have prevented the grant of the patent.

Amending the relevant US patent law could provide a solution to this anomaly. Fortunately in the case of the "turmeric" patent, the Indian government mounted a successful challenge to its validity, citing a 1953 article from the *Journal of the Indian Medical Association* about the use of turmeric as a wound healer. Earlier published (foreign) documents do count as prior art to a US patent.

LACK OF INVESTMENT

This area of concern is the opposite of the first. It relates to large multinationals not investing in creativity arising in developing countries. Countries such as India have good universities and a long and prestigious history of technology invention, but a poor record of exploitation. Part of the reason for this is lack of local capital and/or of inward investment. Another possible reason is that many such countries have historically provided inadequate protection for intellectual property. This historical situation has been radically altered by the harmonizing influences of the TRIPS agreement (see Chapter 2). In his masterful book *The Mystery of Capital*,[5] Hernando de Soto demonstrates why developing countries need modern systems of property to liberate the "dead capital" in their otherwise informally owned land property assets. The thesis can be applied in analogous fashion to the liberation of "dead creative capital" through the use of intellectual property. The difference is that whereas modern property laws are evolving only slowly in these countries, the modern systems of intellectual property arising out of TRIPS are already fairly much in place today.

Establishing systems is one thing, making them work to attract inward investment to local creative business is a different challenge. The inescapable, but not necessarily irredeemable, fact is that the intellectual property systems of developing countries are mainly exploited by foreign multinationals. Developing country entrepreneurs can and should make use of their new systems for protecting intellectual property. As I have argued elsewhere, knowledge (e.g., a new technology) is itself not that valuable, but "fix it" as an asset by the use of intellectual property and it becomes more of a commercial proposition. It is then possible to imagine a scenario where a base technology is developed by an Indian university, protected by an initial Indian patent filing, with inward investment or, indeed, venture capital then obtained for the patented technology. The global internet-based marketplaces for intellectual property described in Chapter 3 are as accessible to India as they are to any other country.

China, the largest emerging market of all, has recently shown great creativity in this area. It has a rich tradition of complementary medicines, but the industrial base supporting this industry is poorly capitalized. Many of the factories are run-down and badly managed. China's solution was to offer limited legal monopoly rights to inward investors in particular areas of complementary medicine. The rights were offered for a set period in return for guaranteed investment. The auction for the rights was even shown on Chinese public television. It was a scene reminiscent of a Sotheby's art auction, with secret parties bidding by phone.

DENYING ACCESS TO TECHNOLOGY

The third area of concern relates to large companies not making technology available to emerging markets, even where in some instances those companies hold patents preventing local companies from using the technology. The truly hot area here is pharmaceuticals, with treatments for major infectious diseases the hottest area of all.[6] This is a complex issue. Some of the factors involved are to do with intellectual property protection, or rather lack of safeguards in that regard.

One big company concern has to do with counterfeiting. What happens if a drug is made available to the developing country and then counterfeits, of dubious medical value, start to appear? Who is responsible for the deaths that might occur of those who use the counterfeit products believing them to be genuine?

Another concern is to do with onward sale of possibly misappropriated genuine product from the intended market to neighboring markets. The concern is amplified if the onward sale results in deterioration of the quality of the product, with the result that the ultimately sold product is defective.

There are competing concerns here of which intellectual property is only a part. Enhanced regulation of drug distribution and better policing of counterfeiting may improve matters. The real challenge, however, may be to do with business model innovation. Two suggestions:

◆ *Create "patent-free" space for certain pharma products.* This could be achieved either through targeted legislation at a local level, or through the big pharma companies simply not filing patents in developing countries. This has the advantage of creating space in those countries for generic drug companies legally to market low-cost copies of the key drugs. Nevertheless, it would have the major disadvantage of keeping big pharma companies out of the developing world. In the longer term, this will be bad not only for big pharma, which loses any opportunity to develop these markets, but also for the countries themselves, which would lose contact with the expertise that international companies can bring, for example as local employers.

◆ *The "low-cost" pharma hub monopoly model.* This is a more radical business model that keeps big pharma engaged, albeit in a non-traditional way. The drug is patented and also trade marked with a "low-cost" mark different to the trade mark used in mainstream markets. Generic companies are granted a patent license on favorable terms and provided with access to development knowhow by the big pharma company, thereby assisting in quality control and keeping development costs to a minimum. The license covers the sale of the patented product in the designated market, but only under the "low-cost" mark, which provides a control mechanism to prevent exports (to mainstream markets). The big pharma company may also require the use of other anticounterfeiting product markings as a condition of the license. This model uses intellectual property in a smart new way to get "low-cost" drugs into the countries where they are needed and keep the big companies involved. One consequence in the longer term could be that the "low-cost" operators grow up to challenge the big players, analogous to the operations of Virgin Atlantic or Southwest Airlines. Enhanced competition may well be another benefit.

PATENTING OF THE HUMAN GENOME

The ethics of patenting genetics research is a major area for debate. Arguably the most controversial episode centers on the sequencing of the human genome. The story begins when J. Craig Venter leaves the $3 billion public and charity-funded official Human Genome Project to set up a competing private company, Celera Genomics.[7] Celera Genomics' business plan also involves sequencing the human genome, in direct competition with the official project. One version of events is that the official project was moving too slowly and lacked energy and drive. Another version is that Venter saw a once-in-a-lifetime commercial opportunity that was too good to miss.

While the official Human Genome Project was set up to make human genome sequence information freely available to the public domain, Celera Genomics is a commercial, for-profit entity. It has established a private, subscription-based database of sequence information, which it has derived itself. It has also patented some of the more important derived sequences. Licenses to the patents will be made available, but not for free. There is a price to pay for speedier access.

There are two points of controversy here. The first is to do with the competing models of public and charity-financed consortium with free, public access to sequence information and privately funded project with access on payment of fees to the sequence information at an earlier date. The second point of controversy is whether the sequence information should be subject to intellectual property protection at all. Surely, the argument goes, the human genome is part of greater human knowledge and should not be subject to private, intellectual property monopolies. President Clinton and Prime Minister Blair seemed to give support to this line of argument when they made a historic joint statement on March 14, 2000 that human genome research "should be made available to scientists everywhere."[8]

However, at least some of the sequence information seems to meet the usual standards for patent and database protection. It is risky, not to say arguably unlawful, for government to make selective exceptions to the usual rules. This is particularly so in an emerging industry that requires confidence in the intellectual property system if further investment capital is to be attracted. And, of course, Celera is making the sequence information available, albeit at a price.

In some ways, it is easy to see Mr. Venter as a maverick opportunist. On the other hand, his actions have led to the human genome sequencing data being made available more quickly to the research community. As long as his license terms are fair and reasonable, with perhaps better terms for less well-funded public institutions than for the better-funded big drug companies, why should he not be rewarded for spotting the commercial opportunity? The message to be taken from this whole story is that private enterprise is the better way to move this industry forward faster, even if that means that licensing fees become due.

As an intriguing footnote, Craig Venter was awarded the title of "Man of the Year 2000" by the *Financial Times*.[9] This recognized his "unwavering determination to achieve his scientific goal" of the decoding of the human genome. So this may really be a story of individual scientific drive, rather than one that is to do with a business model or intellectual property. Only time will tell.

THE IMPORTANCE FOR BUSINESS OF ADDRESSING PUBLIC UNEASE

This chapter has shown how intellectual property is becoming the subject of debate, concern, and even outrage and protest. Business needs to engage positively in the debate and to act responsibly in its exercise of virtual monopoly power at both local and global levels. If it fails to rise to the challenge, there are risks of further press and public relations pressure and direct action by the courts or the politicians. There are both lessons from history and some ominous signs on present-day horizons.

In 1882, at the peak of the last technology revolution and a time of some overexuberance about patents, the US Supreme Court issued a famously robust decision on boat propeller technology. The decision refers to "speculative schemers" who build "patented monopolies, which enable them to lay a heavy tax on the industry of the country, without contributing anything to the real advancement of the arts." What is worrying for the virtual monopoly business is that a recent *Economist* leader article entitled "Who Owns the Knowledge Economy?" chose to dust off that old decision.[10] The article also made reference to the present Microsoft case before the US Supreme Court and warned about "natural susceptibility to monopoly" in a modern, networked economy. Patents are coming under fire. And with certain companies openly advocating and/or practicing strategies of "land grab" and "patenting as much as we can," the press articles will find some justification.

Brands have also been in the front line. A recent book entitled *No Logo*[11] vividly describes the reaction against the growth of brand power. To an extent, whether antibrand trends catch on or not must be contingent on the action of the brand owners. Overly aggressive marketing and/or excessive policing of trade mark rights may well push the balance in the wrong direction.

Given the mood in certain parts of the press, is it any wonder that the politicians feel under pressure to respond? The joint Clinton/Blair statement on the human genome is a disturbing signal of what might happen if business fails to act appropriately. The overall danger is that the new opportunity of virtual monopoly economics may be quashed for purely political reasons before it has had time to deliver its full potential. That would be a disaster for the creative economy.

PART THREE

TOOLS FOR BUILDING
VIRTUAL MONOPOLY

9

ROAD MAP FOR BUILDING
VIRTUAL MONOPOLY

THIS CHAPTER INTRODUCES A BASIC "STRATEGIC ROAD MAP" FOR building virtual monopoly. A nine-point approach is proposed, but it is possible to start at the point that best suits where you and your company are today.

1 BRING INTELLECTUAL PROPERTY INTO YOUR EVERYDAY EXPERIENCE

Here are two views of intellectual property:

Traditional view: Obscure, specialist pursuit, best left to the experts.
Virtual monopoly view: Everyday legal enabler, integral part of business.

Stick with the traditional view and you will never be in a position to help your company build virtual monopoly. To bring intellectual property out of obscurity and into your everyday experience, try some of the following:

◆ *Scan the business press*. This is full of intellectual property stories: "One-click patent injunctions," "Napster mayhem," "Genome patent panic," and so on. Build up a feel for the trends.

◆ *Scan the supermarket shelves.* Look for generic products and patented improvements; branded products and lookalikes; character merchandising; product markings, and so on. Identify the various types of intellectual property in operation.

◆ *Visit websites of major corporate players.* To start with, try Microsoft, Unilever, or Pfizer. Search using "patents," "trade marks," or "copyright" as a keyword. Get a feel how these companies use intellectual property.

◆ *Bookmark the major Patent Office sites.* The US, European, and UK Patent Office sites have a great deal of useful background on the legal basics. Also try www.bustpatents.com for an alternative view of the workings of intellectual property.

◆ *Meet informally with your attorney.* This is not to talk about any specifics, but to understand how they view the scene. Get a feel for the world they inhabit.

I use many of these techniques when giving awareness-raising seminars to business people on the basics of intellectual property. The first 10 minutes are spent on this week's headline stories; there are always plenty. Then we take 20 minutes or so on for the legal basics; the Patent Office websites are great self-help resources for this sort of material. Then the supermarket comes to visit. Out come everyday products—a diaper, a compact disc, a yellow sticky note, a can of spaghetti shapes, an item of fruit—and the audience splits up into teams and has 20 minutes to prepare a presentation on the intellectual property content of that product.

Then comes the "banana test." This asks one simple question: How much intellectual property can be associated with a banana? The marking scheme is as follows:

◆ Blank, slightly embarrassed look—Definite fail.

◆ Discussion of patents for possible genetic modifications, disease resistance technology, storage and transport methods, plus trade marks for brand names such as Chiquita and Fyffes—Definite pass.

◆ Further discussion of Andy Warhol representations, Velvet Underground album covers, banana trade wars—Funky banana pass!

As for banana trade wars, in the mid-1970s bananas were the subject of a major antitrust action in Europe based on abuse of dominant market position.[1] The strength of the Chiquita trade mark and the control of strategic patented technologies were relevant factors. There can be a great deal of intellectual property associated with even an everyday piece of fruit.

2 UNDERSTAND HOW INTELLECTUAL PROPERTY IS AFFECTING YOUR COMPANY

Start with some basic research, along the following lines:

♦ *Collate past company experiences.* Most companies have some intellectual property stories, good and bad. Collect them. Meet the characters, hear the stories, understand what can be learnt. Build up a historical picture.
♦ *Compare your products with those of the competition.* Make side-by-side comparisons. Look for the patented improvements, branded components, and design-arounds or lookalikes. Who is being more creative? What are the effects of intellectual property?
♦ *Survey your intellectual property landscape.* Start with patents, trade marks, and copyright. Get some searches done. Develop an overview of what your company is doing versus your competitors and collaborators.
♦ *Get a feel for the relevant virtual monopoly business models.* Refer to the four virtual monopoly business models outlined in Chapter 3. What models are at play in your business area? Which models are dominant and why?
♦ *Meet with your attorney.* Talk about your work and the specifics of the above research. Get their views. Get a feel for their level of business awareness. How does what they do affect your company at a business level?

This basic research will give you a good overview of where your business is and what the possibilities are. It is now time to start to translate that overview into action.

3 BUILD A VIRTUAL MONOPOLY TEAM

Recall that in the traditional view, intellectual property is an obscure, specialist pursuit, best left to the experts (attorneys, agents, lawyers, solicitors). That view has to date largely determined how intellectual property has been practiced. The chances are that your experts:

◆ Are based distantly from your creative teams (e.g., in head office "cocoons")
◆ Adopt a distinct mindset from your creative teams (e.g., legal, defensive)
◆ Talk differently from your creative teams (e.g., formal, legal jargon).

In the virtual monopoly view, intellectual property is an everyday legal enabler and integral part of the business. Building virtual monopoly therefore requires that intellectual property be wrested from the sole ambit of the experts. An integrated team approach is needed. The experts will continue to be key components of that team. Their special-ist expertise in the handling of statute, rules, procedures, and (above all) documents is invaluable, but other skill sets are also required. Desirable team attributes are:

◆ *Combined skill sets*—Creative, commercial, and intellectual property skills. All team members possess specific expertise and general awareness of one another's areas of expertise.
◆ *Business aware*—Tuned in, a good understanding of the business.
◆ *Knowledge enabled*—Readily able to survey the creative, commercial, and intellectual property landscapes to identify opportunities and risks.
◆ *Communication hungry*—Speaking one another's language, mixing face-to-face meetings with phone, fax, email, whatever fits the need.

The team composition can be flexible, with not all players on the pitch at the same time. Team members may be both company employees and outside experts. Geography does not matter that much. Shared virtual monopoly mindset matters a whole lot more. There is no room for "them and us" or for ways of working that encourage traditional divides. The suggested mindset may be enough to unite all sides—in horror!

4 ADOPT A PROPERTY DEVELOPMENT MINDSET

Building virtual monopoly is about building desirable economic spaces using intellectual property. The virtual monopoly team mindset is therefore that of the property developer. This is a practical, hands-on mindset, which is all about leveraging property value from base knowledge assets. It is not "beanbag creative" or "bookish expert."

The property developer mindset has certain strong characteristics:

◆ *Sense of property.* Property is all about legal title, ownership, and defined boundaries. It is a negative right to exclude others backed up by the force of law. The property developer uses legal ownership to establish boundaries and leverage capital. The virtual monopoly team embraces intellectual property as business currency to leverage intellectual capital.

◆ *Sense of landscape.* The property developer surveys the landscape and is not afraid to explore to find undeveloped niches. The virtual monopoly landscape comprises intangible intellectual property, but can readily be surveyed by electronic means. Undeveloped areas may be gaping wide or niche-like.

◆ *Sense of transformation.* The property developer sees base assets both as what they are and for what they could be. For the virtual monopoly team, the base assets are knowledge based. Transformation in this context means turning ideas, information, and knowledge into intellectual property.

◆ *Sense of opportunity.* The property developer is opportunity focused. Issues may arise, but they are there to be overcome. Contrast this with traditional ways of managing intellectual property that focus on issues. To build virtual monopoly, tradition needs to be turned on its head. Instead, think intellectual property opportunity—the new IPO.

◆ *Sense of portfolio.* The property developer appreciates the enhanced value of a portfolio as opposed to isolated, individual properties. The virtual monopoly team also sees the enhanced value of well-constructed intellectual property portfolios and broad, defensible virtual monopoly spaces.

◆ *Sense of sweat.* Property development is about building, making, constructing things. It is an active, sweat-creating occupation. Building virtual monopoly is also active, but here the sweat has more of a strategic and creative nature.

5 START TO BUILD VIRTUAL MONOPOLY THROUGH AN INITIAL STRATEGY

To build virtual monopoly you need to start somewhere. You won't break into a sweat just thinking about doing it. You need an initial strategy, which to start with is probably best kept simple. Base the initial strategy on a concrete, business result that your company can achieve through the use of intellectual property.

Good straightforward examples include:

◆ Protecting investment made in developing a technology/brand/content
◆ Stopping a competitor from selling a similar product/service
◆ Licensing/franchising ideas to a third party in return for royalty payments
◆ Being seen as a player and requiring visible intellectual property for this
◆ Using intellectual property rights to get better deals with licensed suppliers
◆ Having some bargaining chips to play with if a competitor brings a lawsuit
◆ Creating distinct legal assets to sell off when exiting the business.

None of these initial strategies will be sufficient to enable your company to build virtual monopoly, but all are good reasons for getting into intellectual property. If your company is new to the intellectual property game, use these to justify an initial foray and learning exercise. If, however, your company is an old hand at intellectual property but you still engage in it only for these basic reasons, you need to move things further along.

6 BUILD POWERFUL VIRTUAL MONOPOLY THROUGH CREATIVITY AND DIFFERENTIATION

Technology managers from both large and smaller businesses often ask me: "How can I build a strong, broad patent portfolio for my technology business?" My answer is usually blunt and goes something like: "Develop a broad, strong technology portfolio and the patent portfolio will almost build itself."

Stated more broadly, a strong creative portfolio is at the bedrock of a strong intellectual property portfolio. However, the creativity should not stop there. The virtual monopoly team as a whole should be capable of confidently mixing:

◆ Classic creativity
◆ Business concept creativity
◆ Legal creativity.

The virtual monopoly team achieves interplay between all these creative elements. What results is powerful creativity and differentiation (C&D) in terms of both new product and service business concepts, and legal strategies to develop strong intellectual property around these concepts. This is not the usual way of doings things. The traditional process is a fully arm's-length interaction between, for example, a white-coated engineer in a lab, a reactive defender attorney in a paper-clogged office somewhere else, and a road warrior business development manager in another place altogether.

Business startups may get closer to the required interplay, but they often struggle to get truly creative attorney direction. Virtual monopoly does require legal creativity in aspects such as:

◆ Drafting well-scoped individual patent or trade mark application(s)
◆ Timing applications for strategic impact

♦ Structuring portfolios of applications for breadth, defensibility, and flexibility
♦ Matching the portfolio to the requirements of the business model(s).

Legal feedback can also assist the classic and business concept creativity processes in terms of identifying:

♦ Uncluttered spaces with scope for developing broad virtual monopoly
♦ Niche spaces with scope for developing niche virtual monopoly
♦ Existing rights holders as potential development or alliance partners.

The creative–legal–business interplay within the team will lead to the identification and development of more differentiated, more valuable virtual monopoly spaces.

7 CONSIDER ALTERNATIVE VIRTUAL MONOPOLY BUSINESS MODELS

Chapter 3 introduced the four business models for exploiting virtual monopoly. Here is a reminder of them with some typical areas of business application:

♦ The fortress monopoly model (big pharma)
♦ The value-added monopoly model (consumer products)
♦ The hub monopoly model (technology standards)
♦ The monopoly-in-a-box model (biotech startups).

The chances are that one business model predominates in your industry, but that the picture is different in other industry areas. The reason for the difference may be soundly based, or it may simply be tradition. Consider experimenting with alternatives.

The bigger and broader your virtual monopoly space(s), the more you will be free to experiment. As a first step you may also wish to consider any opportunities offered by the broader trends described in Chapter 3:

◆ The garage sale (large corporations)
◆ The intellectual property marketplace (open to all)
◆ The open house (internet developers).

8 CULTIVATE AND REINVIGORATE THE PORTFOLIO

Imagine that you have now adopted the mindset of the property developer, brought a great virtual monopoly team together, and developed a sound intellectual property portfolio. You are, furthermore, reaping the benefits of desirable virtual monopoly space(s) using a mix of traditional and alternative business models. What more can there be to do?

There are two more areas to consider, portfolio management and portfolio lifetime.

PORTFOLIO MANAGEMENT

Your intellectual property portfolio is costing you money. This is definitely the case if you are paying renewal fees for patents, trade marks, registered designs, and even internet domain names. You will want to manage that ongoing cost, which is not necessarily easy.

The problem with an intellectual property portfolio is that it is virtual in nature. This makes it difficult to work out which parts are of high value and therefore worth maintaining, and which have low or nil value and are probably worth letting lapse. This is a major problem for large corporations that may be spending tens of millions of dollars on renewals each year with no real guarantee that their money is well spent.

It will probably be possible to identify some "crown jewels" that should be maintained at all costs. Some "rogue weeds" of nil value may well also be easy enough to spot. As for the rest, a pragmatic solution is to set a budget and maintain as broad a portfolio as can be afforded. Then, think about a "garage sale" and use this as a way to rechallenge yourself to think about other business models.

PORTFOLIO LIFETIME

Patents have a finite lifetime, generally 20 years. Copyrights do have longer lifetimes and trade marks can last indefinitely, but in buzzy markets the value of an established virtual monopoly space can change rapidly. The big threat is that a creative competitor builds an even more desirable space, and the value simply migrates. Your virtual monopoly space may be under threat already, and you may not realize until it is too late.

The answer is simple. Keep your property developer's hat on and continually add to and reinvigorate your portfolio. Change the layout and nature of the estate if that is where the market is going, or even take a virtual bulldozer to it and start again from scratch. But don't think that it will last forever. That is one of the reasons for its being termed a virtual monopoly: It is not absolute or impenetrable.

9 APPLY "CULTIVATE AND REINVIGORATE" MORE GENERALLY

For those familiar with the writings of Charles Handy, life is a portfolio. You might therefore consider applying cultivate and reinvigorate not only to the intellectual property portfolio, but also to other areas:

◆ *The virtual monopoly team.* Reshuffle, retrain, and give team members the opportunity to explore different property development scenarios.
◆ *Third-party relationships.* Building on the suggestion in Chapter 7, take a portfolio view of your development partners, strategic alliances, and so on. Do not be afraid to get the hedge trimmers out.
◆ *Third-party disputes.* Building on the suggestion in Chapter 6, take a portfolio view of any ongoing intellectual property disputes. Use the tools of cultivate and reinvigorate to develop an optimal "fight–deal–fold" portfolio.

10

BUILDING VIRTUAL MONOPOLY
IN TECHNOLOGY

TECHNOLOGY USED TO BE THE SOLE REMIT OF BIG CORPORATIONS, government, and university research labs or the occasional maverick inventor. However, in recent years technology has broken free and connected with the outside world. It is beginning to define domestic, public, and commercial spaces. Building virtual monopoly in technology is all about the quest to own the commercial rewards offered by control of the technology defining those spaces. This chapter provides practical "strategic tools" for building virtual monopoly in technology.

DRIVERS FOR BUILDING VIRTUAL MONOPOLY IN TECHNOLOGY

The drivers are strong and powerful:

◆ The explosive innovation of the digital-assisted technology revolution *per se*
◆ The new connection between technology and business opportunity
◆ The growth of partnering relationships centered on technology
◆ The opening up of global patent systems
◆ The entrepreneur's desire to develop a future-defining technology.

DEVELOPING PROPERTY IN TECHNOLOGY

Building virtual monopoly in technology requires the mindset of the technology innovator to be interwoven with that of the technology property developer. Any technology not protected by property rights will be commercially less valuable because it is instantly more open to copying. This is true even where the technology is strongly innovative.

Patents are by far the dominant form of technology property, providing new, useful, and inventive technologies with a legal stamp of property ownership.

Subsidiary forms of technology property protection are provided by:

♦ Rights in designs
♦ Copyright in software, databases, or semiconductor masks
♦ Industry-specific rights, e.g., plant/animal variety rights.

The strongest and most valuable technologies combine both property strength and technology.

PATENTS

Patents are the powerhouse. Building virtual monopoly in technology means that the development of patents must be a central part of the innovation process. Patents provide 20 years' legal monopoly protection for inventions that are new, inventive, and useful.

Inventions

These constitute a "technical solution to a problem," which need not be a groundbreaking technology advance. Many inventions are incremental improvements to existing technologies. Examples of types of inventions include:

♦ A mechanical apparatus, device, or mechanism
♦ A chemical or biological compound or composition
♦ An electronic component, system, or software application
♦ A method of making, using, or applying something (in a new way).

New

This means new in the sense of not having been clearly and unmistakably "made available to the public" anywhere and by any means, including publication or oral disclosure before the filing date of the patent. This is an objective requirement—something is either new or it is not.

Inventive

This means "not obvious" to a nominal "skilled person." The skilled person is deemed to have access to all knowledge relevant to the field, but to lack any capability for invention. The concept of obviousness is a subjective requirement, something that many court judgments have considered at length. In general terms, the legal standard for "non-obviousness" is quite low. Fewer patents would be granted if that were not the case.

Useful

This means what it says, although it is sometimes couched in terms of capable of being applied industrially. This is not a big limitation. If the invention is not useful (in some area of industry) it is unlikely to have commercial value.

With all of the above there are nuances, caveats, and points of difference between local legal standards. Any half-reasonable patent attorney will be able to expound on these detailed points. However, in basic terms, you should consider patent protection if you have something that:

◆ Has some technical character (or can be applied technically)
◆ Is useful (somehow, and therefore has commercial potential)
◆ Is new (or is known as such, but applied in a new way).

Do not worry about obviousness, since this is always arguable, but do keep your invention secret until you have filed the patent. Do not worry about all those nuances, caveats, and local points of difference, but do think expansively about all the commercial areas in which the invention may be applied.

SUBSIDIARY FORMS OF PROPERTY PROTECTION FOR TECHNOLOGY

Patents are most of the picture, but not all of it. It may also be worth thinking about subsidiary forms of property right.

Rights in designs

These are particularly relevant where the technology will be realized as a product with a characteristic three-dimensional form. Examples of areas where designs are important include the automotive industry; electronic consumer goods such as cameras; and medical devices. Most countries provide registered design protection, which typically lasts for about 15–25 years. Some countries also provide unregistered design rights or design copyright, with typically narrower protection than for registered designs. Design law lags behind patent law in terms of international harmonization.

Utility models or petty patents

These are available in some countries (e.g., Germany) but not all. These are shorter-term (e.g., 10–15 year) patents for less significant technology advances. They are often granted without any examination formalities and can have value in low-tech, fast-moving industries such as toys.

Copyright and related rights

Copyright protects software, technical documentation, and databases from copying, but not from independent creation of their content. Related rights include specific forms of protection for databases and semiconductor masks.

Industry-specific rights

If these rights are relevant to your industry you probably know about them already. Examples include plant variety rights, animal variety rights, and supplementary protection certificates to extend the lifetime of marketed drug products post patent expiry.

STRUCTURAL FORMS OF PROTECTION FOR TECHNOLOGY

Be aware of relevant structural (i.e., nonproperty) forms of protection, which can provide useful further barriers to entry.

Control of knowledge flow
This is not knowledge itself, but control of the *flow* of that knowledge. In the world of virtual monopoly, knowledge (insight) is expensive to create and readily rendered worthless if it is not carefully controlled or reduced to property form (e.g., by way of a patent). All of the further structural barriers listed below rely on careful conservation of technology insight.

Development and manufacturing capability
It takes time, careful nurturing, and major investment in knowledge to build an organization that is capable of developing "raw technology" into a marketable product. This structural barrier is the most likely reason that most drugs will continue to be developed by a handful of big players, for example, even if drug discovery (and patenting) is becoming an activity for niche startups.

Agreements
The power of an exclusive Agreement should not be underestimated. If you form webs of exclusive partnering relationships with the best co-developers, distributors, or contract manufacturers, you can build up a powerful barrier to entry to any competitor. However, continue to control the knowledge flow to your web. Webs that are too open can leak knowledge.

Regulatory approval hurdles
Many technology products require regulatory approval of some kind. The knowledge-led capability to address these approval procedures provides a further structural barrier to entry.

STAKING AN INITIAL PATENT CLAIM

The patent lifetime of 20 years can be a long time in the world of technology. You will want to stake the best claim possible. Here is a five-point "in a nutshell" guide to staking an initial patent claim:

1 DEVELOP A TECHNOLOGY PROTOTYPE

You can file a patent on a good idea, but a useful time to think about patenting is when that idea has been reduced to a working prototype. It does not need to be a finished product, or even to have been taken to "proof of concept" stage. Sign and date any lab notebooks, experimental data, or drawings of the prototype. Keep everything secret at this stage.

2 PUT THE TECHNOLOGY IN COMMERCIAL CONTEXT

Think around the technology and research the possibilities. Where, how, and why will this technology have commercial value? What are the existing technologies and why is this an improvement? What are the preferred ways of implementing the technology? Build up a picture of the commercial potential of the technology.

3 FIND A GOOD PATENT ATTORNEY

You can write your own patent, and strictly you don't need an attorney. However, the value of your patent will depend on how well it is written and presented to the Patent Office(s). This is a complex, expert area with many traps and pitfalls into which DIY efforts can readily fall.

4 JOINTLY DEVELOP A SET OF PATENT CLAIMS

The most important part of any patent application is the claims, which define the scope of legal monopoly sought. Work together with your attorney to develop a rounded claim set that fully embraces the potential of your invention. Talk through the commercial big picture and let your attorney see any prototypes, drawings, or experimental results.

5 FILE THE INITIAL PATENT APPLICATION

Take advice on procedural aspects. Typical steps involve a search and examination by the Patent Office, amendment and/or argument, payment of various fees at different stages, grant and, in some countries, post-grant opposition. Ask about costs, timings, and the need for further technical input. Look for synergy between the procedures and your business plans. Do you want to go fast or slow? When would it be helpful to have those search/examination results? Try to fit the procedure to your business plans. Later in this chapter, I recommend an optimal synergetic approach.

CONFIDENT CREATORS BUILD BIGGER SPACES (DESPITE THE PATENT CLUTTER)

Building virtual monopoly around a technology requires three basic factors:

◆ Creating new and different technology
◆ Building an intellectual property (patent) position around that technology
◆ Establishing freedom to use that technology.

All of these are interlinked and dependent on the ambient technology and intellectual property environment. You are by now well aware that the patent environment is immensely cluttered. Nevertheless, from Chapter 5 you will also know that confident creation offers a way to beat the crowds.

"Begin with the end in mind" is one of Stephen Covey's "7 habits."[1] Here the desired end is big, broad, and differentiated virtual monopoly spaces. These habits will help you get there:

1 SURVEY THE EXISTING LANDSCAPE

Identify the players, the emerging patent trends, and any breakout technologies. Focus on both the big picture and the attractive niches. Make note of any threats and no-go areas. Create organizational systems to enable the mapping process.

2 EMBRACE THE LANDSCAPE—DON'T BE AFRAID OF IT

Develop a mindset that spots the opportunities, while acknowledging any risks. Build this into the culture of your organization. Stop focusing on patent issues (as most corporate cultures do) and start seeking patent *opportunities*. Mine the technology content of other people's (e.g., your competitors') patents to explore new technology perspectives.

If you want to know the technology secrets of IBM, Nokia, Microsoft, or whoever, read their patents. Play with their ideas. Look for the strategic opportunities that they have missed. However, don't just react to the existing landscape, start to define a landscape all of your own.

3 LEARN TO SPOT CLAIMABLE INVENTIONS AS THEY ARISE

To create patent positions you need to learn how to spot the inventions arising from your own technology efforts. You can read about novelty and inventive steps and all the patent detail, but to bring it alive you need to learn how to spot the arising inventions and claim them effectively. Spotting inventions is partly about beginning with the claim in mind.

As a quick example, I wanted to learn how to claim "business method" inventions. I assembled a collection of the pioneering Amazon, Priceline, and Walker Digital business method patents. This gave me a good idea of what this new area was all about and what sort of claims the (US) Patent Office would accept.

4 FILE SOME "PRACTICE" PATENT CASES

You learn by doing. Identify some initial claimable inventions and work with your attorney on preparing the patent claims. File at least one case, and use this as a learning exercise. This may seem frivolous, but over the years I have noted that with most inventors their best patent is not their first one. Mandy Haberman's patent for the Anywayup cup was not the first patent she had filed. Similarly, James Dyson's dual-cyclone vacuum cleaner patent followed on from many earlier patent filings on wheelbarrows and the like. Edison filed thousands of patents. Some of them weren't that earth shattering, but I'll bet that the major ones built on learning from the earlier cases.

5 UNEARTH THE "INVENTION BEHIND THE INVENTION"

One of the tests that sorts out truly powerful inventions from those that are merely run-of-the-mill is whether the invention is capable of giving rise to further spinoff inventions. Think about different uses, or perhaps applications in other commercial areas.

A powerful example is provided by Procter & Gamble's transfer of the basic moisture absorbency technology developed for diapers to its Always feminine hygiene product. Always went on to become a megabrand. If you find it difficult to identify any inventions behind your invention, then you either need more legal creativity or the invention has limited utility.

6 VIEW THE INVENTION AS A TECHNOLOGY CONCEPT

The word "invention" is quite narrowing. It has mechanical product overtones, which in a world of digital systems and networks is slightly incongruous. If you view a product invention not just in terms of its component features, but also in terms of its methods of use or modes of application, the concept will broaden out.

For example, a phonecard for a "pay as you go" mobile phone is something mechanical (i.e., a paper or plastic card), but it is also a gateway to a larger telecommunications system. Technology concept thinking will help you see the bigger spaces.

7 VIEW THE TECHNOLOGY CONCEPT AS A BUSINESS CONCEPT

What business model will allow you to extract value from this patented technology? Think of all the options and develop patent claims that give you flexibility within that model. For example, if the invention has three principal areas of commercial application, write independent claims to each area. Then if you want to assign or license those claims separately it will be more straightforward to do so. Even consider writing business method patent claims for aspects of the business model itself. If the technology can be implemented as part of a web-based system, this kind of claim is almost certainly available.

8 VIEW THE BUSINESS CONCEPT AS A BRAND

Use the patented technology as the starting point for building a powerful brand space. Many of the classic power brands used a new technology to build a brand. And whereas patents die at 20 years, brands can live forever. Examples already mentioned are Tide (the first synthetic detergent), Crest (the first fluoride toothpaste), and Pampers (the first disposable diaper). Think as well about Pentium microprocessor chips or iMac computers or, indeed, the Anywayup cup.

Let me close with a strong example of confident creation as a whole. I have been deeply impressed by Microsoft's confidence in seeking to redefine the computer games landscape with its Xbox games console. That landscape is presently "owned" by Nintendo and Sony Playstation. The graphics and sound technology of Xbox are reputedly state-of-the-art and deeply patented. However, Microsoft has clearly also viewed the technology as a business concept and the business concept as the Xbox brand.

0 ... 12 ... 30 ... PCT BLAST OFF! A ROAD MAP FOR CONFIDENT CREATORS

Now that you have acquired the habits, you need a specific road map for building virtual monopoly in technology. The "0 ... 12 ... 30 ... PCT blast off!" road map shown in Figure 1 is a four-stage process for creating synergy between the processes of confident technology creation and international patenting.

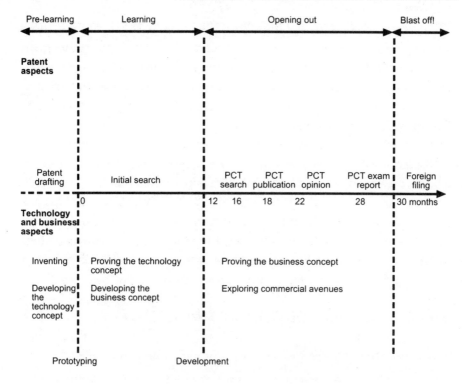

Figure 1 The 0 ... 12 ... 30 ... PCT blast off! road map

STAGE 1 PRE-LEARNING (< 0 MONTHS)

The starting points are invention, technology concept development, and prototyping. In tandem, some freelance patent searching and market understanding are conducted. Everything is kept secret at this stage, from all except your patent attorney with whom you work to create a rounded set of patent claims. A first patent application is filed at your local Patent Office requesting that it does a prior art search. The filing date, the date on which the initial patent claim is staked, is "0 months."

STAGE 2 LEARNING (0–12 MONTHS)

Now that the patent is first filed, you have 12 months to develop its true potential. The Patent Office search should be back in 3–6 months, which will give you a good idea of the prior art picture. In the meantime, focus on enhancing the basic technology and prototypes. Also get to grips with developing the business concept, including branding aspects. Think about how you want to take this forward. Do you want to manufacture yourself, or outlicense, or merely create a monopoly-in-a-box to sell on? Where and who are the markets?

You may need to involve expert consultants or development partners in this learning process. If you do so, it will be on the basis of a situation where you already have a basic patent "stake in the ground." The development partners may want to cut an equity deal with you, but hold back on that for now. You are still learning, still building value, and it is too early to share the spoils. The end-point for the 12-month learning stage is a major updating of the patent filing with all the learnings, which is filed as an international PCT patent application.

STAGE 3 OPENING OUT (12–30 MONTHS)

This is the busiest stage, both in terms of legal and commercial aspects.

Legal aspects

The PCT patent procedure enables you to keep your patent options open for a further 18 months (i.e., to 30 months from first filing) in more than 100 countries (including US, Japan, and all of Europe) on the basis of one application. The procedure also provides:

◆ A good prior art search (at about 16 months from first filing)
◆ A patent publication (at about 18 months from first filing)
◆ An Examiner's opinion as to patentability (at about 22 months from first filing)
◆ An opportunity to amend the application (after the opinion)
◆ An Examiner's report as to patentability (at about 28 months from first filing).

You can, if you want, jump ship after the search and before publication, thereby keeping your invention secret. However, a common approach is to let the patent publish and then respond to the Examiner's opinion, either arguing against the objections or amending (e.g., limiting) the claims to meet the legal requirements (usually novelty and inventive step). A good objective is to try to get a positive Examiner's report to assist with international patenting in Stage 4.

Commercial aspects

While all this legal stuff is going on, you have 18 months to engage in exploring commercial avenues for the technology. If you are thinking of teaming up with a big player, or seeking venture finance, or just selling the concept to colleagues in the commercial part of your corporation, you can use the PCT procedure to help you. For example, make use of a positive search or opinion as validation of the distinctiveness of your technology. Use the timelines to leverage any negotiations or deal making. The main objective here, with good reason, is that you get to a clear direction on commercialization before the 30-month date.

STAGE 4 BLAST OFF OR BAIL OUT (> 30 MONTHS)

The good reason is that once you reach 30 months you come to what is known as the PCT National Phase decision point. At this time your single PCT patent application dies, but can give rise to multiple patent filings in as many of those 100 or so countries in which you wish to gain protection. If you want to maintain broad coverage it can become very, very expensive since you are dealing with concurrent national (or supranational) patent procedures, fees, even translation costs. The good news is that if your Examiner's report is positive, this can cut down the complexity and cost of any later national examinations. Many countries simply accept the substance of the PCT Examiner's Report.

Variations on the "0 … 12 … 30 … PCT blast off!" procedure are used by many of the major technology companies. One advantage for the smaller company in adopting the same road map is that you equip yourself to compete, engage, or deal with the majors on their terms. The road map can be further tailored to fit specific commercial situations, but I will leave your patent attorney to talk you through the details. Other procedures can also be considered such as those focused only on your home market or region, but these inevitably limit any global ambitions.

PATENTING COSTS AND THE SMALLER TECHNOLOGY COMPANY

One disadvantage of patenting is the costs involved. Here are ballpark patenting costs for a technology of moderate complexity.

"0 ... 12 ... 30 ... PCT blast off!" road map costs:

◆ Stage 1	Patent drafting and searching	$3–7,000
◆ Stage 2	Revamp patent and file PCT application	$5–7,000
◆ Stage 3	PCT examination and responses	$3–5,000
◆ Stage 4	National Phase filings (per country)	$3,000
◆ Plus	National exam, grant, renewal costs	Variable

Single-country patent costs:

◆ Stage 1	Patent drafting and searching	$3–7,000
◆ Stage 2	Patent examination and responses	$1–3,000
◆ Plus	National grant, renewal costs	Variable

Initially the "PCT blast off!" and single-country costs are similar, but keeping international options open comes with a price tag. The costs can be slimmed down slightly if you do most of the legwork yourself, or indeed made a lot bigger if the technology is complex or if you use a major-league law firm. However, injecting some realism as to patenting costs is a good discipline. If you are a small company and these costs seem high, then probably patenting isn't for you.

KEEPING CONTROL OF RELATIONSHIPS WITH DEVELOPMENT PARTNERS

Technology is rarely developed without outside assistance, in the form of development partners who provide specific expertise. As noted in Chapter 7, these relationships are often fraught with intellectual property squabbles. To minimize the risk of diluting your patent position while enabling the relationship to add value, I suggest the following:

◆ *First put a stake in the ground.* Don't even think about contacting a development partner until you have filed a patent on the technology. That way you will ensure ownership of at least the basic patented concept. I often refer to the advice of that sage of relationships, Woody Allen: "Always write your name in your books before moving in to live with somebody." If it all goes sour at least you are sure to get your books back!

◆ *Don't give your knowledge away.* Set up a confidentiality Agreement (nondisclosure Agreement) before you give a potential development partner any details at all about why you want to work with them. Beyond that, apply the rules of "need to know." Only give them information that they really need to have. At the first meeting this may amount to nothing confidential, since what you are likely to be most interested in at this stage is whether they have the skills/ability to be able to help you. Initially, let them do most of the talking.

◆ *Agree who will own arising intellectual property.* Before working with the development partner, sign an agreement dealing with not only confidentiality, but also with who will own arising intellectual property (mainly patents) and knowledge. If they won't sign, don't work with them unless there really is no one else who can help you. During the relationship continue carefully to control the outward flow of knowledge/insight.

◆ *Be open about patents,* but only as open as you need to keep the relationship on track. Pass on any copies of published patent applications, which after all are in the public domain in any case. Beyond that, agree ground rules and ensure that everybody sticks to them.

A fast-growing part of my practice relates to disputes involving technology development partners. Think ahead, follow the above suggestions, and you will be more likely to have a productive development relationship rather than one in which you need an attorney to sort out the arguments.

PATENT RESOURCES AND FURTHER READING

On the patent strategy side, I have on my bookshelf *Rembrandts in the Attic*,[2] *Patent Strategies for Business*,[3] and *Patent Strategies for Researchers and Research Managers*.[4] For the basics of patenting I recommend *Patents for Chemicals, Pharmaceuticals and Biotechnology*,[5] which is international in perspective and more broadly useful than the technology-specific title suggests.

For up-to-date descriptions of (ever-evolving) procedures, I recommend visiting the websites of the United States,[6] European,[7] Japan,[8] and United Kingdom[9] Patent Offices and the World Intellectual Property Organization[10] (PCT procedures). For context and attorney contacts, try the websites of the American Intellectual Property Lawyers Association[11] or the Chartered Institute of Patent Agents (UK).[12]

11

BUILDING VIRTUAL MONOPOLY

IN BRANDS

TWENTY YEARS AGO BRANDS WERE LARGELY ENCOUNTERED IN THE supermarket. Tide, Crest, Crackerjack, Cheerios, Pepsi, and Marlboro—these are the traditional face of branding. Well-established, consumer goods oriented, and safely confined to your local Wal-Mart until placed in a shopping cart and ultimately allowed access to your home. Today it is all very different. From training shoes to online banks, from drugs to computer chips, from toilet paper to internet service providers, brands demand our attention in all areas of commerce. This chapter describes the drivers and provides practical "strategic tools" for building virtual monopoly in brands.

DRIVERS FOR BUILDING VIRTUAL MONOPOLY IN BRANDS

Business has not embraced branding without good reason. There are specific drivers:

◆ The need for business to differentiate itself in ever more crowded marketplaces
◆ The realization that added business value may be created through branding

- ◆ The realization that buzzy, open-access marketplaces can assist in the establishment of new and different sorts of brands
- ◆ The emergence of new kinds of products and services where the brand is the dominant value component.

DEVELOPING PROPERTY IN BRANDS

Building virtual monopoly in brands requires adoption not just of the mantle of the brand creative, but also that of the brand property developer. Any brand that is not protected as property will be commercially weaker because it is wide open to copiers. This is so even where the brand works well in the market.

The principal form of property protection is provided by trade marks, a legal stamp of ownership indicating the origin and quality of the product or service to which the brand is applied.

Subsidiary forms of protection are provided by:

- ◆ Internet domain names
- ◆ Registered company names
- ◆ Copyright
- ◆ Unfair trading practice laws.

The most valuable brands combine both property (mainly trade mark) strength and creative/emotional character that works in the marketplace.

TRADE MARKS

Trade marks are all about distinctiveness, that is, the capability to distinguish something in the marketplace. In trade mark terms there are two kinds of distinctiveness, absolute and relative.

Absolute distinctiveness

This is essentially about the trade mark not being descriptive of the relevant branded goods or services or any characteristic of them. Strongly distinctive marks include purely invented words like Kodak, Exxon,

Xerox, Adobe, and Zeneca. At the other end of the scale, descriptive marks include things like a telephone logo for a telecoms business, or "Marlow Travel" for a travel agent based in the English town of Marlow, or "Hot 'n' Spicy" for Indian food.

In practice, most marks are somewhere between absolutely distinctive and absolutely descriptive. Many marks allude to (but do not describe) the goods or services in question. Examples are Microsoft for computer software, Vodafone for mobile telecommunications, or Palm for a (smart) personal data assistant. There is a skilful balance between providing a creative allusion to the goods/services and not having a descriptive mark. As a minor complicating factor, in some countries a borderline descriptive mark can acquire distinctiveness through extensive market use. Evidence of market use and acquired distinctiveness needs to be provided, which can be an expensive and uncertain process.

Relative distinctiveness

This is essentially about the trade mark being distinctive relative to any other mark registered for the same or similar goods or services. A mark with relative distinctiveness is one that in the mind of the average consumer of the relevant goods/services is not identical or confusingly similar to any earlier mark. It stands out from the crowd.

The test for confusing similarity is not a simple one, since it depends on a comparison of the relevant marks and the relevant goods/services as viewed by the relevant average consumer. Pragmatic commercial factors may also be relevant, such as who owns the earlier potentially "similar" mark and how widely they are using it. Widely used and well-known marks are likely to have stronger protection. And (wealthy) owners of well-known marks are more likely to defend their existing trade mark positions with vigor.

What is great about a trade mark is that once validly registered it can have an unlimited lifetime, provided that it is used in the course of business. The potentially infinite payback lifetime is a huge incentive to invest in strong brand monopoly based on strong trade mark protection.

What can be registered as a trade mark?

A trade mark can be any sign capable of graphic representation that can distinguish the goods/services of one party from those of another. The mark can be a word such as Apple, a graphic device such as a stylized picture of an apple, a slogan such as "Apple Stimulates the Fruits of Creativity," or indeed a color, a sound, or a smell. In practice, the vast majority of trade marks are words or graphic devices, but there are odd examples of other types of mark. For example, in the Community Trade Mark Office an application has been filed for "the smell of fresh cut grass" for tennis balls.[1] In the US, Harley Davidson tried to register "the exhaust sound of applicant's motorcycles, produced by V-twin, common crankpin motorcycle engines when the goods are in use," but this trade mark application has since been abandoned.[2]

Applying for a trade mark generally involves submitting a formal application for registration in each particular country or region. The application indicates the class of goods or services to which the mark will be applied. There are 34 classes of goods but only 8 classes of services. In the emerging world of branded services that 34:8 ratio begins to looks something of a historical anomaly.[3] Procedures differ, but often involve a search and examination of the application for absolute or relative distinctiveness or for both. Use of the trade mark is also important, since in almost every country if you do not use the mark within a set period (generally five years), the registration can be revoked for non-use.

SUBSIDIARY FORMS OF PROTECTION FOR BRANDS

Trade marks are by far the most important kind of intellectual property for protecting aspects of brands. Nevertheless, there are other legal and commercial tools that can be used to strengthen brand monopoly positions.

Internet domain names

These can be registered online at low cost and with minimal effort. Most companies try to register at least the .com domain name and the domain name relevant to their country, such as .co.uk for the UK or .de for Germany. Internet domain name registration is organized on a "first come, first served" basis. If the relevant domain name is already taken, consider very carefully how this will limit future electronic business options. It goes without saying that this is an important consideration for almost any company.

Company names

These can also be registered at low cost but provide little by way of effective protection. In most countries, the principal motive for having a company name registration procedure is merely to create a defined, legal trading name for a company. Nonetheless, if your brand is a corporate brand (i.e., based on the company name), securing company name registration will be important.

Copyright

Any content relating to the brand, including packaging, advertising in any medium, trade literature, manuals, product descriptions, etc., is likely to be subject to copyright. Keep copies and good records of all content, including early drafts. In the event of direct or me-too copying of the brand by an infringer, a legal cause of action in copyright infringement may be available. Those good records may prove invaluable.

Unfair trading practice laws

Many countries have legislation relating to unfair trade competition that protect businesses from instances of unfair trade practices. These laws can sometimes be used effectively against direct copiers, lookalikes, or me-too brands. In the UK, for example, there are common law rights in "passing off" that can be asserted against third parties that seek to misrepresent or pass off their business as yours in a way that damages established business goodwill.

The classic case in the UK involved a lemon juice product sold under the name "Jif Lemon" in a yellow, plastic lemon package. A competitor also selling lemon juice under a different name, but in a similar lemon-shaped pack, was deemed by the House of Lords to be unfairly passing off. Reliance of unfair trading practice laws should not, however, be seen as a substitute for strong trade mark protection.

CREATE SPACE WITHIN THE BRANDSCAPE

As you will now be beginning to appreciate, succeeding at creating strong virtual monopoly based on brands is about three aspects:

◆ Creating a brand name and/or logo that is distinctive of the goods/services in which the company intends to trade. The brand name/logo most probably alludes skilfully to those goods/services in a consumer-relevant way.
◆ Creating a brand name and/or logo that is distinctive relative to any earlier marks for goods/services identical or similar to those in which the company intends to trade. The brand name/logo should be equally distinctive in all relevant marketplaces.
◆ Building a strong trade mark position around the distinctive brand name and/or logo. This third aspect is clearly contingent on the first two.

The first aspect is largely under the control of the brand developer. The second, by contrast, requires research into the existing competitive trade mark landscape in each marketplace of interest. That landscape comprises both the Official Register of trade marks in each marketplace and the marks actually used there.

Researching the Official Registers and usage of marks is relatively straightforward. Most trade mark advisers will be able to assist with electronic searches and this need not be wildly expensive if only a limited number of countries is involved. Finding available trade mark spaces in the increasingly crowded brand landscape can be a real challenge, however.

What the research is most likely to uncover is a "traffic light" picture of risk presented by earlier existing marks. This is particularly likely to be the case in the most crowded brand areas, such as computer software, printed publications and clothing.

◆ *Red means stop.* If the search shows that a major company has registered and is using the brand name that your company wants to use for your goods/services and in your chosen markets, the risk profile is definitely "red." Choose another brand name. Do another search. This is frustrating, but if you proceed on red the most likely outcome is that the major company will threaten and/or sue you for trade mark infringement. That will prove hugely more expensive than a quick brand redesign.

◆ *Green means go*. If the search shows no competing earlier marks, you have a "green" light. Proceed with registering your mark and get ready to use it in the confidence that you are occupying a distinctive brand space that you will soon own by virtue of your trade mark.

◆ *Amber is the most likely color*. This is where the search shows a mixed picture of possible risk from competing earlier marks. Many factors come into play. The first are legal factors: How close is that earlier mark? What is the likelihood that a court would regard your chosen mark as distinctive to the earlier mark? For example, is Viagra for pharmaceuticals similar to Viagrene for male health tonics?[4] What about Viagrene for male aftershave? The second set is market factors: Is the proprietor of that earlier registered mark actually using the mark? If not, can it be bought off them for a nominal fee? Or indeed, is there a chance that the mark is invalidly registered? Can the mark be revoked for non-use? Then there are corporate risk factors: Is the owner of the earlier mark a big player or a small company? Is it worth taking a risk, accepting that this may mean facing a dispute at some later point? Dealing with amber is where a good trade mark adviser can really help you.

CONFIDENT CREATORS DEVELOP TRULY DISTINCTIVE BRANDS

Is there a secret to maximizing the chance of getting to green with fewer shades of amber? The answer is yes, and it comes back to creativity. Truly differentiated marks with a strong air of distinctiveness are likely to get to green more often. Combined with strong consumer relevance, these differentiated marks are in turn more likely to result in valuable brand monopoly.

As evidence, let us consider a recent survey of top brands.[5] Of the most valuable five brands, Coca-Cola, Microsoft, Intel, and Nokia inherently possess a strong air of distinctiveness. These marks would stand out even if you were encountering them for the first time. IBM, which is an acronym for the rather descriptive International Business Machines, is the outsider, or possibly the exception that proves the rule.

THE BRAND MONOPOLY MATRIX: A ROAD MAP FOR CONFIDENT CREATORS

Distinctiveness is at the heart of creating virtual monopoly through brands, but this is only one factor in what is a matrix process. The brand monopoly matrix shown in Figure 2 provides a road map.

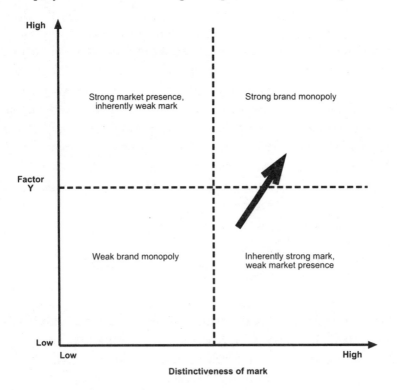

Figure 2 Brand monopoly matrix

The distinctiveness of the mark (both absolute and relative) is shown on the x-axis as the first key factor. Thus, a nondistinctive mark such as Candy Treat for a confectionery product would be on the far left end of the x-axis, and a distinctive mark such as Hersheys would be on the far right end of the x-axis. The y-axis represents the second key factor, Factor Y, which comprises a whole range of components such as:

◆ Creative character of the mark
◆ Consumer appeal of the mark
◆ Care and nurturing of the mark over time
◆ Marketing spend
◆ Marketing strategy and creativity
◆ Product quality.

Factor Y is a complex entity. What is refreshing for the smaller company is that spend is only a part of it and probably not the most important part. Looking at the brand matrix:

◆ The most desirable position is the top right-hand quadrant, characterized by strong distinctiveness of mark and strong Factor Y. For examples, think any of the real power marks such as Louis Vuitton, Gillette, Chanel, Rolls-Royce, and Dell.
◆ The bottom left-hand corner is the least desirable position. These are the marks that you probably haven't heard of and even if you did you probably wouldn't remember them.
◆ The bottom right-hand quadrant is a good place to start. Here you have a distinctive, registrable mark and with added Factor Y you can transition into the strong brand monopoly top right-hand quadrant. Indeed, the arrow shown on the diagram is probably the ideal track for a new brand. The mark starts out reasonably distinctive, but it is not a meaningless, invented word. It already has some Factor Y in the form of creative character and consumer relevance. Think about Playstation, Palm Pilot, Pampers, and even Microsoft or Intel in the early days. With some added Factor Y in the form of marketing spend and strategy, the top right quadrant will soon be in reach.

◆ The top left-hand quadrant, characterized by a strong market presence but inherently weak mark, is the one to avoid. It is very difficult, even with huge market use, to turn an inherently weak mark into a strong one. If the reason for the mark's weakness is absolute, i.e., it is a descriptive term, that is going to be very difficult to overcome.

AVOID THE TOP LEFT-HAND QUADRANT OF THE BRAND MATRIX

Two real-life examples will illustrate why you should avoid the top left-hand quadrant.

Microsoft has struggled in many countries to register Windows as a word trade mark for its very well-known software product. To some eyes, Windows is a descriptor for software involving a window-like graphical user interface. For the current status of the Windows trade mark in your country, search the Official Register of trade marks.

The Czech company Budvar Budjevecky and Annheuser-Busch of the US have had long, seemingly endless battles over the mark Budweiser in the UK and elsewhere in Europe. The origin of these particular battles dates back to events at the time of the Second World War that created relative weakness in the Budweiser mark. The weakness persists because there are competing beer products, each with historical local rights in the Budweiser name. As both players have sought to expand globally, the relative weakness has been exposed and running conflicts have resulted. Just as a trade mark can live forever, so apparently can messy trade mark disputes.

Two basic points:

◆ If your company finds itself in the top left-hand quadrant, it is largely because of decisions made about the brand in the early days of the business. The message is clear: Think about the brand monopoly matrix from the beginning. Start at the right point on the distinctiveness x-axis and with added Factor Y the desirable top right-hand quadrant will become available in time.

◆ Once you find yourself in the top left-hand quadrant it is difficult to escape. Adding Factor Y and moving upwards in the matrix are not that hard, although they may be expensive. Adding distinctiveness and moving sideways are much more difficult, although possible. Consider IBM in the early 1960s trading under the clunky banner of International Business Machines. It made the decision to rebrand by getting Paul Rand, one of the finest graphic designers of that and any time, to design the now famous "split-line" IBM logo.[6] In consequence, IBM moved sideways and strongly into the top right-hand quadrant. Microsoft, perhaps responding to the difficulty in registering the Windows word trade mark, developed the well-known Windows ("flying toast") logo, which is a registered trade mark. You may have noticed how Kentucky Fried Chicken is trading as the (inherently more distinctive) KFC. Is there a sideways shift in progress here as well?

BRANDING MODELS

There are various different models of branding:

◆ *Corporate brand.* Here the name of the company is the brand name. It is used on all corporate literature and probably on all products. Think about Unilever, General Electric, and Cisco Systems as examples of strong corporate brands.
◆ *Product/service brand.* Here the brand is applied to a product or service. Tide, Crest, Pampers, and Always are examples of product brands. The product/service brand may be used on its own or in conjunction with the corporate brand name. If used purely on a standalone basis it may make it easier to sell off the brand as a separate asset in the long term.
◆ *Umbrella brands.* Think about McDonald's various "Mc names" for its different fast food products or Heinz 57 food varieties. The umbrella brand acts as a unifier for the full product range.
◆ *Brand brands.* These are the brands that almost seem to have an existence of their own. The brand essentially is the product. Think about Pokemon, Tommy Hilfiger, or possibly even Napster.
◆ *Portal brands.* These define a branded consumer entry point. Classic examples include shop brands such as Macy's or Harrods. Emerging

examples include online stores such as Amazon or internet portal sites such as Yahoo! or AOL.

◆ *Hub brands.* These are like portal brands except they define not an entry point but rather a hub component of a larger product. This may be a technology hub component such as a computer chip or operating system. Think about Intel Inside or Bluetooth or ARM-powered or Linux. The branded technology hub adds major value to the product, which itself essentially becomes a box for the branded hub component inside. But also think about a content hub such as *The Lord of the Rings.*[7] The starting point is J.R.R. Tolkien's classic trilogy of books, but now there is also the movie, the website, and the video game; the book has spawned a brand.

◆ *Character brands.* A character brand uses the name of a famous person for reasons of endorsement. Examples would include Ralph Lauren's Polo and Linda McCartney's vegetarian foods.

Of course, generating maximum value from brands is all about matching the branding model with the profit-generation model of the overall business. Think about how to match the branding model to the virtual monopoly business model. Some matches are straightforward, e.g., hub brand and hub monopoly model. Others require greater virtual monopoly team insight.

BRANDING MATTERS REGARDLESS OF COMPANY SIZE

While it is true that many large, successful businesses excel at branding, trade marks can create significant value for smaller companies and need not cost a fortune. Here are two classic reasons for any company (large or small) to benefit from creating virtual monopoly in brands:

◆ Protecting investment made in developing a brand
◆ Stopping a competitor from selling a similarly branded product or service.

Other more subtle reasons include:

◆ *Creating a brand name distinct from that of the business founders.* This is very relevant to any entrepreneur who sets up their own business and finds that inevitably much of the goodwill and value in the business is tied to their own name. Establishing a separate brand not linked to that name can make an exit strategy much more straightforward.

◆ *Creating a brand name derived from that of the business founders.* This is the opposite of the previous reason. Examples would include Louis Vuitton, Benetton, Gucci, Rolls-Royce, Saatchi & Saatchi, or even McKinsey.

◆ *Creating distinct trade mark assets with which to sell or trade.* It is becoming much more common to regard brands as separate trade-able assets. In the UK, for example, the Ford Motor Company now owns the Aston Martin, Jaguar, and Land Rover car brands.

◆ *Being seen as a market player and requiring trade marks for this.* Many companies like to register trade their mark so that they can use the symbol ®, which means "registered trade mark," as opposed to ™, which merely means "trade mark," usually unregistered and probably weak.

◆ *Using brands to get better deals with suppliers/distributors.* This is a factor in any department store. The best positions in the store go to the bigger brands.

◆ *Franchising a branded business to a third party in return for a royalty payment.* This is a hugely popular business model these days. Franchise agreements are often structured around the licensed use of one or more registered trade marks. Many other terms relating to product quality, supplier selection, staff training, etc., will also be present, but the trade mark license is the controlling factor.

BRANDING THE SMALLER COMPANY

A personal example: I set up my own firm of patent attorneys some years ago. I initially thought about using a corporate brand model, but decided instead to follow the more traditional route and trade under my own name as "Pike & Co." I did, however, invest in a professionally designed corporate image and logo and registered the domain name www.pike.co.uk. In the last couple of years the corporate image has been incorporated in both brochures and a much expanded website. The overall cost has probably been $8,000 over the years. In terms of intellectual property protection, I have trade mark rights on the logo, an internet domain name, and copyright on content such as the logo and website.

Recently, I decided to establish a strategic consulting arm focused on the business uses of intellectual property. I was braver this time and adopted a branded approach. The brand name selection process essentially involved brainstorming about 200 names ranging from descriptive to totally invented. I wanted to add some Factor Y, so I focused on names that had a degree of creative character but also customer relevance. These tended to incorporate the letters "IP" or "IPR," which are well-known abbreviations for intellectual property and intellectual property rights respectively.

I shared the shortlist of names with various friends and colleagues and eventually came up with two favorites, IPEX and IPRICON. Both are inherently distinctive, invented words. In terms of Factor Y, IPEX incorporates three out of four letters of my earlier business name (Pike) and the fourth letters, x and k, are phonetically similar. It lends itself to straplines such as "Intellectual property expertise" or "excellence" or just "ex" (i.e., out there), and it is short, snappy, and difficult to spell incorrectly. IPRICON offers the Factor Y that it is a conjoining of IPR and the word "icon," which would give rise to some nice iconic logo opportunities.

To check on the third-party risk picture I searched both generally on the internet and on the Official Registers of trade marks in the US and UK. Both marks were available for my business area of interest, although IPEX is also the brand name of the International Print Exhibition and of a US-based piping business. In the end, I plumped for IPEX. I registered the IPEX word trade mark in three classes in the US[8] via the USPTO online registration process and in five classes in the UK,[9] where the class fees are cheaper. Securing a relevant domain name was not easy, but I did register www.ipex-uk.com; not ideal, but acceptable. I then had a simple website designed that imports some of the character, particularly the colors, of the earlier Pike & Co. corporate image. The total cost was probably 60 hours of my time and $5,000. Not peanuts, but not huge bucks either.

In business terms, the return on investment in design, logo, and web-site for Pike & Co. has been tremendous in terms of positive customer response. The money was certainly very well spent. In terms of IPEX it is still early days, but with registered trade mark rights the payback life-time is potentially long.

BRAND RESOURCES AND FURTHER READING

Many books and articles are published on emerging brand trends such as e-branding,[10] internet branding,[11] technology branding,[12] and pharma branding.[13] For the bigger picture, I often refer to Interbrand's excellent book *Brands: The New Wealth Creators*[14] and the companion volume, *Trademarks*.[15] For good basic guidance on brand creation, Al and Laura Ries's no-nonsense *The 22 Immutable Laws of Branding*[16] is well worth a look.

For a description of trade mark procedure (like patents, ever evolv-ing) I recommend visiting the websites of the US,[17] Japan,[18] and UK[19] Patent Offices, the Community Trade Mark Office,[20] and the World Intellectual Property Organisation.[21] For context and attorney contacts, try the websites of the American Intellectual Property Law Association[22] or the Institute of Trade Mark Agents (UK).[23]

12

BUILDING VIRTUAL MONOPOLY
IN CONTENT

F OR CONTENT READ COPYRIGHT, SINCE THIS IS THE DOMINANT FORM OF intellectual property in content. Copyright, the most widely created and most widely abused form of intellectual property, has risen from obscurity to become headline news. Indeed, the headlines are creating new dictionary definitions, from "digital piracy" to "napsterization" to the rather intriguing "warez," downloadable software (often pirated) for sale via the internet. This chapter shows you how to build virtual monopoly in a world where it begins to seem impossible to protect almost anything. First, we need to put context behind the headlines.

THE LIBERATION OF CONTENT

The content industry includes popular films, television, music, books, magazines, porn, computer games, fashion design, etc. By contrast, copyright concerns the protection of literary, dramatic, musical and artistic works—and there lies part of the problem. In origin, traditional copyright is a somewhat quaint, even idealistic construct protecting "works" rather than industrial-scale "content." It used to work well because up until the 1950s the disseminators of works tended to operate on a small scale within defined markets. However, then everything began to open up into a mass market of pop music, soap operas, high-street fashion, home videos, cable and satellite television, and computer games. A larger-scale content industry emerged as the provider of many channels of content in diverse media forms. In tandem, niche providers of specialist content came into being. And the internet exploded on to the scene as a construct enabling anyone to become a content provider. The problems currently faced by copyright result, in part, from the liberation of content to its present state of extreme accessibility.

If the liberation of content is the driver, technology has been the enabler. The tools of copying have been around a long time, from the printing press onwards, although they have become more available since the 1960s, from the Xerox copier to the VHS video recorder to the killer combination of PC with internet access and CD burner.

By way of an extreme example, sales of music singles fell by 46 percent in the US in the year 2000, a drop that many linked to the "Napster effect."[1] Napster is a file-sharing technology that enables computer users to share music content rapidly, at low cost, and potentially to disregard any relevant copyright or royalty obligations. Nevertheless, it is people, not technology tools, who make illicit copies. In a world where content has become something for the people and the tools of piracy are available to the people, to safeguard its existence the copyright industry must win the hearts and minds of the people. In part, Napster took off because music fans objected to paying high industry prices for music CDs. One real challenge for the company seeking to build virtual monopoly in content is to secure popular consent for its models of business.

DEVELOPING PROPERTY IN CONTENT

Copyright is the principal form of protection for content. It provides protection for any literary, dramatic, musical, and artistic works that are original in their expression and recorded in some way. The standard for originality is low — marginally above "not copied" is not too far from it. In many countries copyright comes into being on creation of the original work and there is no explicit requirement for registration. As a result of international agreements such as the Berne Convention and the

Universal Copyright Convention, the protection is automatically extended to most countries.

Copyright has a long lifetime, although the complex rules can make it difficult to determine exact lifetimes for particular works. Count on a lifetime of at least 70 years for most works, sometimes much longer.

Examples of copyright works include:

◆ Works of fiction (e.g., novels, screenplays)
◆ Works of description (e.g., newspaper articles, photographs)
◆ Works of instruction (e.g., recipes, computer programs)
◆ Works of art (e.g., paintings, sculptures)
◆ Works of fashion (e.g., fabric and costume design)
◆ Works of drama (e.g., films, plays)
◆ Works of collation (e.g., guide books, compilations)
◆ Works of publication (e.g., books, websites).

The range of works open for protection is immense, as is the potential for different types of copyright work to exist in a single product. Think of any newspaper, in which there will copyright in the published form (e.g., layout), in the individual articles, in any quotes from other sources, in any photographs, and in any advertising material. To add to the complexity, each copyright may have a different owner or be subject to different licensing terms.

Ideas, expression, and the house of cards

Copyright protects the expression of an idea, rather than the idea itself. This is why competing newspapers can legitimately run different versions (expressions) of the same news stories (ideas) without any problem. Copyright only provides a monopoly against copying of the expression of an idea, but not against the independent creation of that same expression. So if by chance (and not by copying) two newspapers independently come up with the same headline, there is again no problem in copyright.

The idea/expression dichotomy can leave a major gap in the protection that copyright provides for truly original and different works. That gap has become the enabler, or at least the established mode of business, of whole swathes of the content industry, from fashion design to "black box" computer game writing.

Creative designer Hilary Anderson comments that even the vocabulary of the fashion industry has been shaped by this gap. Truly original and distinctive "signature" works act as "influences" for the mass market. Commercial designers are often asked by manufacturers to design along the lines of an earlier work — not to copy the expression, of course, since that would infringe copyright, but certainly to be influenced by the original idea. The overall effect on the industry is a rapid filtering down of original, authentic, signature works into me-too products. The originality of the signature creator's work becomes diluted, as does their share of the market benefits. Why bother to be original?

Hilary shared with me her experiences of seeking to create an original signature style. The new look was inspired by the idea of assembling, in collage form, personal collections of artefacts, hand drawn in near-photographic representation and set against rich backgrounds of burnished colors. The feel of the collage compositions is classical and authentic — the London V&A museum collection meets Italian still-life line drawing on a warm, autumnal evening.

The look was created as a personal project, but while in New York Hilary took the opportunity to show her portfolio to selected stand-holders at a major exhibition. One of them, Beryl Isherwood of Design Line, saw the opportunity to use the works as greeting cards. A marketing deal was struck and the cards became a significant commercial success. About a year later, Hilary was surprised and perhaps a little flattered to discover me-too versions of cards employing the collage look on the shelves of a local shop. Flattery turned to annoyance when she subsequently met a commercial agent openly using her cards as an "influence."

Nevertheless, as she admits, this is "all part of being in the industry." It is also a product of the idea/expression gap, which can make copyright protection something of a house of cards. Hilary's advice:

> "Keep striving for originality, but do keep things confidential for as long as possible. That way you will at least beat the me-toos to the market."

OTHER FORMS OF PROPERTY PROTECTION FOR CONTENT

Other legal aspects of protection for content include the following.

Digital copyright legislation

In existence in the US and rapidly on its way in Europe is legislation that significantly toughens the range of measures available to prevent digital piracy, both legal and technological. This is copyright with a big stick, if you like. It has been applied by the courts in the US to curtail Napster's activities. Already some people are asking if the legislation goes too far, while others question whether it goes far enough.

Database rights

These are available in some but not all countries. They protect databases (e.g., in digital form) that take investment in time and effort to create, but that do not necessarily result in original copyright works. By way of example, database rights protect both the content of the standard telephone directory (alphabetical listing) and the *Yellow Pages* (more original/skillful format). Infringing acts can include unauthorized extraction and use of significant amounts of data content.

Moral rights

These are not available everywhere. They protect creators of works, by for example requiring a publisher to name the author of a published work at the time of publication. They also protect against unfair or derogatory treatment of works.

STRUCTURAL FORMS OF PROTECTION FOR CONTENT

The world of content is, in general, a world of low barriers to entry. However, some of the structural (i.e., nonproperty) forms of protection in Chapter 10 may be configured to provide additional entry barriers.

Control of knowledge flow

If you can keep the next "big story" secret until you publish, you gain first-publisher advantage. The newspaper "world exclusive" is the best example, but it could also be a lifestyle book on the next major home design concept.

Editorial capability

In a world where content is liberated and potentially dumbed down, editorial capability matters more. It takes time, careful nurturing, and significant investment in knowledge to build an organization that is capable of developing raw ideas into quality content. This structural barrier is one reason that I expect to be reading the *Wall Street Journal* in 50 years' time, even if financial information is freely available on the internet.

Distribution agreements

Channels of content distribution matter. Control those channels by way of exclusive partnering relationships with the best distributors (e.g., cinema chains, bookshops, or online portals) and you can build up at least an initial barrier to entry for any competitor.

DEVELOPING ENFORCEABLE RIGHTS

Developing property in content gives rise to enforcement challenges that are less prevalent in the worlds of technology and branding. However, if the recent Napster decision is taken as a guide, the (US) courts are still on the side of the copyright owner.

Here are some sensible steps that any property developer will want to take:

◆ *Keeping good records of creative output.* Copyright requires no official registration, but you will need to demonstrate the existence and ownership of copyright if you want to take action against illicit copiers. Keep very good records of any creative output, including early drafts and demos.
◆ *Marking of all creative output.* Mark all creative output with the © symbol, the author's name, and the date (usually the year) of creation. This marking will assist your record keeping, and it is also an assertion that you own copyright in the work, to remind any potential copiers that it is yours.

◆ *Agreements.* Make sure that all agreements with employees, consultants, development partners, etc. include clauses relating to ownership of copyright. It is almost impossible to think of a professional or creative relationship that will not result in the creation of copyright work. Ensure that you retain ownership or at least access to those works.

◆ *Set traps for copiers.* Think about how to trap unauthorized copiers. Here is one idea: If you are creating a customer database, why not add in some dummy entries. That way if the database is copied you can counter any "independent creation" defense by reference to the copying of those dummy entries. Even better, why not give the dummy address as that of your lawyer, so that if any material is sent to that address as a result of copying (which may happen without your knowledge) you can detect it and take action.

CAN CONTENT BE PROTECTED IN A DIGITAL WORLD?

It is time to address the big question. Below are three different views.

NO: COPYRIGHT IS DEAD

This view is becoming surprisingly popular, particularly among close observers of the digital revolution.[2] There are a number of strands to the argument:

◆ *Ideas and knowledge should be free.* This is absolutely right, and copyright does not protect knowledge or ideas, only their expression as works. Accepting free flow of ideas does not mean that copyright loses its economic purpose as a legal property right subsisting alongside the ideas and knowledge.

◆ *Copying of the content, which embodies ideas and knowledge, should also be free.* In the world of copyright this is not so. Nevertheless, most copyright laws incorporate "fair dealing" rights enabling individuals to make limited numbers of copies (usually one) of copyright works for personal, noncommercial use. Additionally, if content providers wish to waive their rights in copyright they are free to do so.

◆ *In the days before copyright people still used to create great works.* This is true, but most relied on patronage or were poor. Neither of these economic models is likely to be particularly popular today.

◆ *The professions (e.g., lawyers, doctors, architects) do not rely on copyright.* This is true, but they do rely heavily on structural and regulatory barriers of entry to their professions, not to mention hefty fees.

YES: TOUGH LEGISLATION AND ANTICOPYING TECHNOLOGY ARE THE ANSWER

This view also has its followers and in some ways the wind is blowing in their direction, even if they face an opposing hurricane of digital piracy:

◆ *Digital copyright legislation and the recent Napster decision* undoubtedly give support to view that tougher legislation is the answer. However, tougher laws do not always work. Prohibition did not stop people wanting to drink alcohol in the 1930s. And there is little sign that the public mood is entirely anti-Napster.

◆ *Technology is available to prevent digital copying.* This is true. One example is the Digital Property Rights Language developed at Xerox PARC. Nevertheless, this technology is likely to be too expensive to apply to all content channels, even if we are only talking a couple of cents a throw.

MAYBE: BUT ONLY IF ALL BUY INTO THE BENEFITS OF COPYRIGHT

This is my view, and I was pleased to find some alignment in a recent article in *Red Herring* entitled "Digital Content Wars: Can't We All Just Get Along?".[3] Here are some facets of the argument:

◆ *Copyright is imperfect, but it is a reasonable framework for protecting investment in content.* So many major industries (e.g., software, publishing, broadcasting, etc.) and creative individuals depend on copyright as the currency for their models of business that it is highly dangerous to pronounce it dead. Alternatively, if copyright law becomes too rigid, new models of working, engendered by the digital revolution, become more difficult to explore. This will stifle both business concept innovation and individual creativity.

◆ *People don't expect free lunches.* This applies to the general public as much as to the business world. There is no general expectation that content should be free. However, fair pricing and/or innovation in charging models are expected. If you try to sell CDs at inflated prices, don't be surprised if many people tape copies from their friends. If you start to distribute music via online downloads, recognize that people will expect to share in the reduced transaction costs. On the other hand, if a newspaper is on the web for free viewing, most people don't mind putting up with some banner ads, however annoying they are.

◆ *The low-lying fence argument.* If you want to experience a complex world of inadequately fenced-off property, just walk down any suburban street. Those low-lying, white-painted fences aren't really going to present much of a barrier to anyone with a wish to trample over the neat gardens. Nevertheless, most people, for reasons of personal or professional ethics, will respect the boundary and not take advantage of someone else's property. Copyright is like that low-lying fence—easy to jump over, but visible and inviting respect. If this sounds a little quaint, idealistic even, that is exactly where copyright comes from.

CONFIDENT CREATORS USE CONTENT TO LAUNCH VIRTUAL MONOPOLY

Building virtual monopoly in content is possible, but the inherent problems with copyright make it doubly important to bring in other factors. Here are some models that use content as a launch pad.

THE CONTENT DEFINES THE BRAND MODEL

Almost every brand uses content in some form to become established. This model takes it further. Content that defines the nature and quality of the brand is made available on a loss-leading basis. Branded products or services are then sold at premium price. An example would be the publishing output of consulting firm McKinsey & Co., which is either published in leading journals or made freely accessible on its website. The payback comes through consulting business.

Individuals can also operate the same model. Leading management writer Gary Hamel can in some ways be regarded as a "guru brand." His writing is published through many channels, whereas his "boot camps for revolutionaries" are more premium events.

THE CONTENT LAUNCHES THE BRAND MODEL

This is a variation, less subtle but more prevalent. Most people are aware of media merchandising and brand spinoffs. The movie becomes a two-hour commercial for the merchandising. The spinoff action toy or computer game grosses more than the movie. The primary content loss-leads sales of the branded product.

THE HUB SUBSCRIBER MODEL

Subscriber models are becoming flavor of the month after the internet "bubble." Those based on giving many subscribers (flat-rate) access to a copyright-protected content hub are talked about most, as a way to make money from the internet (something that "content is free" is unlikely ever to deliver). AOL is leading the way by offering a content-enhanced internet access service. A dusted-down Napster, allied with German media group Bertelsmann, is also proposed as a subscriber music hub.[4] The model uses copyright licensing as the legal basis for the subscriber relationship.

This model can be taken further, however. Imagine a situation where you hold a patent on the next "industry standard" file-sharing hub. You can bet your bottom dollar that the big players of the established music industry wish they owned patents on the Napster, Gnutella, or MP3.com file-sharing technology (a shame they didn't get round to inventing it).

THE PRIVILEGED SUBSCRIBER MODEL

This model is most applicable to business-to-business markets. Think about a firm that creates a specialist management training program or suite of computer software tools, each subject to copyright. The market for these products is likely to be highly focused, with customer expectations not merely for using the copyright material, but also for hands-on assistance and ongoing support. The subscriber relationship here will be tighter and based on a tailored copyright license (e.g., number of users, features licensed) together with agreed support obligations.

THE BASIC PRODUCT FOR FREE, PAY TO UPGRADE MODEL

Think about the Adobe Acrobat Reader, which you may have downloaded for free from the internet. If you want to upgrade to the more comprehensive Adobe Acrobat package, you have to pay for it. This is on the face of it a pure copyright model, but the free download is also part of a smart exercise in brand building.

THE LIBERATION OF BOOK PUBLISHING

Book publishing is the one area that, until very recently, remained immune from the radical changes sweeping through the world of copyright. Even today, much of book publishing still operates on a small scale within markets largely defined by geographic area. Many publishers tend to operate only in one country and achieve global reach through networks of locally based distributors or publishing alliance partners.

This situation exists because of cultural and language factors, but it survives for other reasons. Copyright plays a part in one of them. Global publishing markets are often divided up along geographic lines on the basis of contracts finding their legal basis in copyright and exclusive publishing rights. This market segmentation enables book publishing to cope with the logistical problem of distributing a niche product, of some bulk (i.e., weight), to a highly dispersed, diversified, and fickle market.

There are inevitably also structural barriers to entry inherent in a divided market. However, the rules are changing:

♦ *Online book stores*. These enable individuals to browse the book stores of the world to find both a publisher's edition and a price suiting their pocket. The cost of shipping books worldwide remains the one factor tending to favor purchase from a local store rather than an overseas competitor.

♦ *Digitalization*. In the digital world, the shipping charge is zero. The market for e-books and print on demand is in its infancy, but if and when these digital forms of book publishing take off, it will surely mean the end of local preference based purely on cost of delivery.

♦ *Parallel imports*. The existing geographic segmentation is based on exclusive licensing and publishing agreements. Laws designed to assist the free movement of goods naturally undermine such agreements. In the European Union, once a product is legitimately placed and sold in one EU state, any intellectual property rights therein are deemed to be "exhausted." Onward sale by parallel import to another EU state cannot generally then be prevented by assertion of intellectual property rights. In global terms, a battle rages between those championing the global freedom of movement of goods based on "international exhaustion" versus those favoring national-based intellectual property rights. The detailed arguments are beyond the scope of this book, but the onward march of globalization must be apparent to all.

What is the book publishing industry to do? My view is that rather than fighting against the trends, it should embrace the opportunities offered by online marketplaces, digitalization, and globalization. The barriers to entry provided by the old segmented structures will surely break down, but confident creation, particularly in the use of branding, offers a way forward.

In a world of extreme access, editorial capability must also matter greatly. Those publishers that add significant editorial value to consistently create differentiated and authentic offerings will be well placed to thrive as global brands. Editorial reputation will, in turn, act as a magnet for the best authors.

Business models will matter more and subscriber models may come to the fore. I can imagine myself signing up to receive all the books released by a leading-edge business publishing "hub" brand, much for the same reasons that I subscribe to the *Harvard Business Review*. Even a privileged subscriber model (e.g., books + seminars + online networked chat rooms with the authors) could have its attractions. More off-the-wall models, such as "the first few chapters free, then pay for the rest," might work; this has in fact already been tried by Seth Godin, for his book *Permission Marketing*.[5]

In a digital world, the old logistics hassles of distribution should weigh less heavily and there will be little practical need for geographic segmentation. Copyright may well end up mattering less, but branding will matter more. And branding thrives not on segmented markets but rather on global reach and distinctiveness.

COPYRIGHT RESOURCES AND FURTHER READING

So much is being written about copyright and digital piracy in the press that my basic advice would be to buy almost any authoritative newspaper or business magazine. Esther Dyson's *Release 2.0: A Design for Living in the Digital Age*[6] is a thoughtful review of the big picture economic issues. The collection of articles in *Caught in a Web: Intellectual Property in Hyperspace*[7] is wide-ranging and captures the present sense of the chaotic. *Digital Property*[8] is good on the practicalities of using copyright to do business in the digital environment.

13

BUILDING VIRTUAL MONOPOLY

ORGANIZATIONS

T HIS CHAPTER SUGGESTS HOW LARGER ORGANIZATIONS CAN BE structured to build and liberate major intellectual property value by organizational focus on virtual monopoly.

CLOSE ENCOUNTERS OF A CORPORATE KIND

Building virtual monopoly is all about the close encounter of classic, legal, and business concept creativity described in Chapter 9. In many traditional corporations the encounter is less close, less joined up. Let me offer two simple models for those who would like to bring the essence of a virtual monopoly organization to their corporation.

ATTORNEY SERVICE OF THE THIRD KIND

A really intriguing model comes from Hugh Dawson, Vice-President, Pharmaceutical Patents at GlaxoSmithKline:

> "*I envisage my team of intellectual property attorneys as piloting a speed-of-light, corporate space cruiser. Our mission is to find and make contact with arising sources of technology insight throughout the company and to apply our expertise to create intellectual property opportunity therefrom.*"

This image of a legal power team cruising at light speed round the corporation actively looking to create intellectual property opportunity from arising technology is truly different from the traditional view of the corporate attorney as a reactive, defense force. The joined-upness comes through an almost entrepreneurial approach to the attorney role.

THE INTELLECTUAL PROPERTY COMPANY WITHIN

Described in Chapter 4 are some pioneering organizations that live, eat, and breathe intellectual property value creation. But an intellectual property company need not be a discrete company. It can be the shared mindset of a network of individuals in a large corporation who work together as an intellectual property company within the larger corporation. The network may also encompass the structure of an intellectual property company in one of its various forms.

FORMS OF INTELLECTUAL PROPERTY COMPANY

There are only two important structural features:

◆ A close link between classic creatives and their intellectual property advisers to form an intellectual property generator
◆ A close link between the intellectual property generator and one or more intellectual property value liberators.

Beyond that the forms are essentially flexible, although there are three common types as shown in Figure 3:

◆ *One to many* — One generator feeds in to many value liberators. This is the original Edison, Menlo Park model. It is also the model of a character-creating company such as Disney, which liberates value by merchandising through many carefully selected licensees. One powerful generator spawns many different avenues for value liberation.
◆ *Many to one* — Many generators feed in to one value liberator. This is probably a reasonable description of the relationship that big pharma

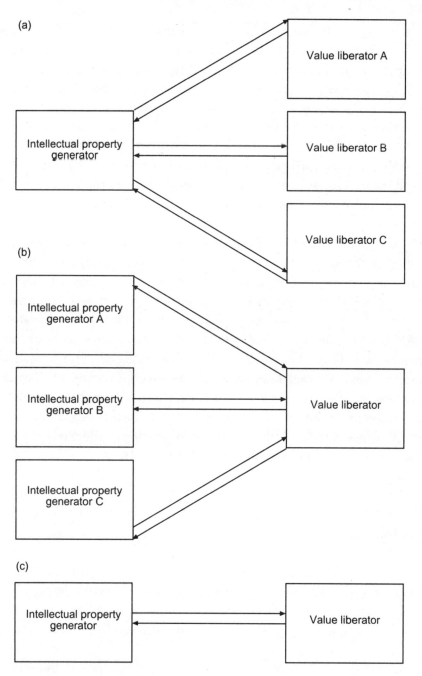

Figure 3 (a) one-to-many intellectual property generator to value liberator relationship; (b) many-to-one relationship; (c) one-to-one relationship

today has with many of the "baby biotech" companies. Each baby biotech company acts as an initial generator of a patented, but unproven therapy that is fed into the big pharma development organization by way of a development partnering relationship.

◆ *One to one*—One generator feeds into one value liberator. This is essentially the model applied by ARM and by Celera Genomics. This also, in part, describes the classic creative or R&D organization where, however, the feed is traditionally a creative feed rather than an intellectual property feed. Intellectual property input is applied at some point as a "value add" but not as a key driver.

All of the above structures separate the intellectual property generation side from the value liberator. This separation can be valuable, since it puts a break between the sometimes emotional area of creativity and the necessarily harder-edged area of commercial exploitation. The degree of split and the balance of decision making can be varied. In alternatives the balance of power may rest in the hands of the creative, legal, or commercial executives. At one extreme, you can imagine a creative entrepreneur CEO wanting to keep very close overall control of both the intellectual property generator and the value liberator. At the other extreme, you can imagine a big corporate with the sole objective of generating finance from a "garage sale" selloff of surplus intellectual property wanting to make the split as stark as possible.

EVOLVING VIRTUAL MONOPOLY ORGANIZATION STRUCTURES

Unless your company is a startup, the creation of a virtual monopoly organization structure should be seen as an evolutionary process. The evolutionary pathway moves from the "classic creative" to "intellectual property company" to "virtual monopoly" organization structure.

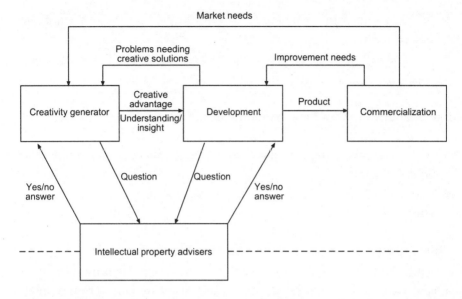

Figure 4 Classic creative organization structure

CLASSIC CREATIVE ORGANIZATION

The structure of the classic creativity-driven organization, be it a technology, design, or brand-driven organization, looks like that shown in Figure 4. There is a central value pathway that takes creative advantage, develops it into a product, and then commercializes that product. There is a primary feedback loop ensuring that the creative effort is guided by market needs, and secondary feedback loops ensuring that any necessary product improvements or problems are given creative attention. The creative and development space is narrowly defined, probably as a result of hemming in by third-party intellectual property.

Intellectual property advisers are available throughout the process and provide input when requested. Generally, the input is in the form of formal yes/no answers to questions. In highly structured companies the creative pathway will often be configured to ensure that these questions are asked at defined decision points along that creative pathway. Example questions at the creative stage are:

◆ Is this technology patentable? Yes = file patent. No = do not file patent.

◆ Is this mark registrable? Yes = file trade mark. No = do not file trade mark.

Example questions at the development stage are:

◆ Is the technology free for use? Yes = OK, go ahead. No = problem to solve.

◆ Is this mark available for use? Yes = OK, go ahead. No = problem to solve.

What must be noted about the classic structure is that intellectual property is an "add-on" to the creative pathway in which it features largely as a barrier gate. The classic structure should result in the creation of intellectual property and in the avoidance of major intellectual property issues. However, the lack of close encounters between the creative pathway and the intellectual property function will prevent the development of significant virtual monopoly spaces. Over time, the intellectual property portfolio may even start to develop independently of the business.

Part compensation for this can be achieved by increasing filing numbers in general "toolup" fashion. However, in the end the intellectual property portfolio will become so large and so divorced from the business that there will be scope to have a "garage sale" of unwanted assets.

INTELLECTUAL PROPERTY COMPANY ORGANIZATION

As shown in Figure 5, this also has a central value pathway, but this is now centered on deriving value from intellectual property through development and commercialization. The creativity center and intellectual property advisers work so closely together that they form an intellectual property generator. All of the yes/no questions previously dealt with at barrier gates in the classic structure are handled as an integral part of the intellectual property creation process.

The resulting output to the development and commercialization functions is therefore creative advantage, strongly protected by

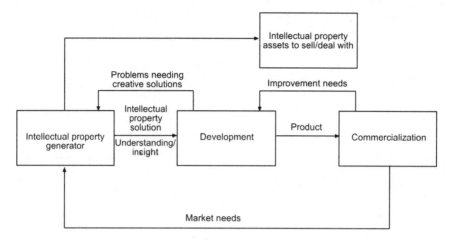

Figure 5 Intellectual property company organization structure

intellectual property and essentially free from third-party intellectual property risk. Again, however, the creative and development space is quite narrowly defined. The primary and secondary feedback loops are still in place to ensure appropriate guiding of the intellectual property generator.

A second commercialization strand has also now appeared. This comprises "spare" intellectual property assets to sell, or to use in leveraging deals with suppliers or as bargaining chips in the event of disputes.

VIRTUAL MONOPOLY ORGANIZATION

This has the structure shown in Figure 6. Again, the central value pathway is centered on deriving value from intellectual property. The starting point is the intellectual property generator. This is relatively small in size and highly skilled, not just in creating intellectual property but also in identifying and building desirable virtual monopoly positions. The development space is thus hugely enhanced. Indeed, this company owns so much desirable intellectual property that it is seen as defining the industry road map.

Any tussles with third parties are readily brushed off. This company has a huge number of options and valuable intellectual property to deal

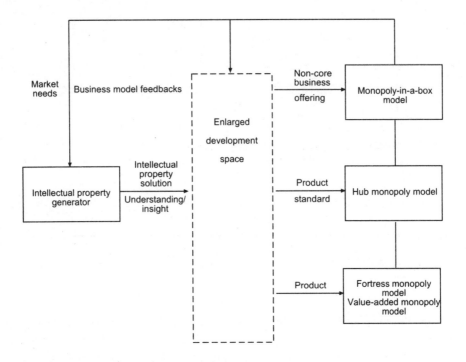

Figure 6 Virtual monopoly organization structure

with to resolve any arising disputes. The broad development space feeds into multiple business models, which may be operated simultaneously if desired. Product feeds are exploited through fortress and value-added monopoly models. Product standards are defined and exploited through hub monopoly models. Non-core product business offerings are exploited through monopoly-in-a-box models.

Indeed, one product of this company should be other companies. It may get so large and powerful that it has to split simply to avoid becoming too large or, perhaps, even to avoid government action enforcing a split. What company or companies (there aren't many) are you now thinking of?

AFTERWORD

WHEN I STARTED WRITING THIS BOOK IN SUMMER 2000 IT WAS CLEAR that intellectual property was becoming a hot topic. The press swarmed with stories of the "napsterization" of the digital environment, patent land grab strategies, brand warfare, cybersquatting, and much more besides. I felt, however, that in focusing on the sexy, controversial stuff, the press headlines were missing the bigger, more fundamental shifts.

By now, you will have absorbed my view of the big picture, one shaped by virtual monopoly islands of exclusivity based on powerful, differentiated creative advantage and sealed in by intellectual property. You will also have appreciated that those islands need not be isolated, static entities. The use of intellectual property in dynamic fashion as the enabler of business models and company structures is all part of the radical shift brought about by virtual monopoly.

Throughout the last year, I have watched as the corporate landscape has been reshaped by the power of virtual monopoly. Witness, for example, those mergers and acquisitions breaking out all over the world of pharmaceuticals and the life sciences. The giants are not merely teaming up to save costs and additional bulk will certainly not make them any more nimble or flexible. These mergers are driven by a desire to bring together desirable virtual monopoly spaces in the form of patented drug pipelines, gene databases, and blockbuster brands.

For example, Merck announced a $620 million deal to acquire Rosetta Inpharmatics,[1] a genomics company with riches almost entirely in the form of intellectual property. The fundamentals of virtual monopoly, rather than atoms of controversy, are starting to define the headlines.

"Will the real monopolist please stand up?"
This question heads up a recent lead article in *Red Herring*,[2] which predicts the forthcoming "duel" over "control of the internet consumer."

The key protagonists are Microsoft, whose Hailstorm web services package is designed to build on its current dominance of the PC environment, and AOL Time Warner, the newly merged king of content.

The battle will have many components; virtual monopoly will certainly be one of them. View this as a battle between Microsoft's virtual monopoly in technology (and brand) and AOL Time Warner's virtual monopoly in content (and brand). The market will decide on the final outcome, but the strength and character of their respective islands of exclusivity will inevitably shape the battle tactics.

Xerox announces its long awaited fight-back strategy

Two key components of this strategy are reassertion of the Xerox brand and a new emphasis on exploiting Xerox's exclusive technology space around high-speed, digital color copiers.[3] Such copiers will be the engines for the "print on demand" revolution and Xerox claims to have 400 patents pending on the technology drivers. The company will also seek to develop new solutions and document services businesses. The new Xerox will embrace an open, knowledge-sharing culture at a grass roots level that encourages sharing of learning, customer feedback, and best practice.[4]

The Xerox example highlights a new paradox: Companies are embracing both virtual monopoly, with its emphasis on exclusivity and intellectual property, and the knowledge economy, with its emphasis on knowledge sharing. As noted in this book, the interface is not always an easy one, because the property "fix" culture of virtual monopoly is almost the opposite of the knowledge "flow" culture of the knowledge economy. Balancing the competing demands of fix and flow is going to be a significant challenge for the larger creative companies in the future. Tradeoffs are inevitable, and will be sometimes painful.

So should you "flow" it or "fix" it? I believe that many companies will embrace the paradox and do both, but that the smarter ones will apply careful strategic controls. If you fix too firmly then you will miss out on the undoubted benefits of knowledge sharing within the company, with alliance partners, and with customers. However, if you let it all flow too freely you run the risk of seeing your most valuable knowledge assets flow out the door.

Here's my vision: The creative company of the future will combine a strong, defensible intellectual property center with fluffy, relationship-building knowledge edges. Think of virtual monopoly islands of profitable exclusivity with great knowledge surf beaches. This probably describes the new Xerox, with its tight control of the brand and 400 patents on high-end color copier technology, but emphasis on practical knowledge sharing at a grass-roots level.[5] It also describes how Microsoft developed Windows 2000 through its so-called embrace and extend approach.[6] Selected major partners were granted access to the source code (the knowledge part) of beta-test versions to try out and play with, on condition that they did not modify the program or reuse the code (the proprietary part). The partners gained some of the benefits of an open source approach and presumably a better final product. Microsoft acquired much valuable feedback and free checking for bugs.

Virtual monopoly island, knowledge beach is the new paradigm. Build property and surf freely. Mix and match the hybrid to fit your company style and ambitions, while accepting that there will be trade-offs. Strategically, I would advise building a strong, powerful virtual monopoly first and then surfing around for those further knowledge gains. Then start building your next, even more desirable virtual monopoly island!

NOTES

FOREWORD

1 *Electrolux v. Dyson*, [1999] ETMR 903.
2 *Dyson Appliances Ltd v. Hoover Ltd*, decision of the UK High Court, October 2000.

CHAPTER 1

1 "The 21st Century Corporation," *Business Week*, August 28, 2000, p. 75.
2 Jack Trout & Steve Rivkin, *Differentiate or Die: Survival in Our Era of Killer Competition*, John Wiley, 2000.
3 Andrew McAfee, "The Napsterization of B2B," *Harvard Business Review*, Nov–Dec 2000, pp. 18–19.

CHAPTER 2

1 James Dyson, *Against the Odds*, Orion Business, 1998.
2 Stephen Van Dulken, *Inventing the 20th Century*, British Library Publishing, 2000 (includes a description of the Monopoly board game patent, US Patent No. 2,026,082).
3 "IBM: Awarded Record Number of US Patents," FT.com, 12 January 2000.
4 *Agreement on Trade-Related Aspects of Intellectual Property Rights, Including Trade in Counterfeit Goods (TRIPS)*.
5 "New Patent Rules Up to Standards," *China Daily News*, September 2, 2000.
6 *The Patent Co-operation Treaty*, Geneva, 1978.
7 *The Madrid Protocol*, Geneva, 1989.
8 *The Patent Law Treaty*, Geneva, 2000.
9 European Community Directive No. 89/104 on the harmonization of trade mark laws within the European Community.

CHAPTER 3

1 Douglas K. Smith & Robert C. Alexander, *Fumbling the Future: How Xerox Invented, Then Ignored, the First Personal Computer*, iUniverse.com, 1999; Michael Hiltzik, *Dealers of Lightning: Xerox PARC and the Dawn of the Computer Age*, Orion Business Books, 2000.

2 W. Brian Arthur, "Increasing Returns and the New World of Business," *Harvard Business Review*, July–August 1996.

3 United States patent no. 4,237,224.

4 "Venter Capital," *Red Herring*, June 2000, p. 296; "Patent Panic," *Red Herring*, July 2000, p. 203; "The Selfish Geneticist," *Financial Times*, December 30/31, 2000.

5 "Protein Powerhouse," *Red Herring*, October 30, 2000, p. 137.

6 "Cosmetic Giants Look to Collar Wave of Start-ups," *Financial Times*, December 30/31, 2000.

7 "IBM: Awarded Record Number of US Patents," FT.com, 12 January 2000.

8 Kevin G. Rivette & David Kline, *Rembrandts in the Attic: Unlocking the Hidden Value of Patents*, particularly Chapters 3 and 5, Harvard Business School Press, 2000.

9 The IBM Patent Server, now known as the Delphion Intellectual Property Network server at www.delphion.com.

10 "Little-understood BTG Aims to Harness Profit Power of Ideas, *Times*, October 23, 2000.

11 The IBM Patent Server, now known as the Delphion Intellectual Property Network server at www.delphion.com.

12 Marcel Corstjens & Marie Carpenter, "From Managing Pills to Managing Brands," *Harvard Business Review*, March–April 2000.

13 Financial Times Survey, Pharmaceuticals, *Financial Times*, 30 April.

14 Douglas K. Smith & Robert C. Alexander, *Fumbling the Future: How Xerox Invented, Then Ignored, the First Personal Computer*, iUniverse.com, 1999; Michael Hiltzik, *Dealers of Lightning: Xerox PARC and the Dawn of the Computer Age*, Orion Business Books, 2000.

15 Kevin G. Rivette & David Kline, *Rembrandts in the Attic: Unlocking the Hidden Value of Patents*, particularly Chapters 3 and 5, Harvard Business School Press, 2000.

16 By way of a postscript, Xerox has recently announced that as part of a broad review of its core operations it is seeking partners for its PARC laboratories: "Investors Set to Scrutinise Xerox's Core," *Financial Times*, March 7, 2001.

CHAPTER 4

1 ARM Holdings plc, Annual Report 1999.
2 Russell L. Parr, "Intangible Assets Dominate Hidden Corporate Value," Chapter 4 of Bruce Berman (ed.), *Hidden Value – Profiting from the Intellectual Property Economy*, Euromoney Publications, 1999.
3 Paul Israel, *Edison: A Life of Invention*, John Wiley, 1998.
4 Ibid.
5 "The Role of Intellectual Property and Patent Information in Successful Innovation, Production and Marketing. Case study I: The Non-spill Drinking Vessel," *World Patent Information*, 23(1), pp. 71–3, 2001.
6 The Anywayup trade mark is registered, e.g., as Community Trade Mark Registration no. 318246.
7 Gary Hamel, *Leading the Revolution*, Harvard Business School Press, 2000.

CHAPTER 5

1 "Patent Wars," *Economist*, April 8, 2000, pp. 95–99.
2 Kevin G. Rivette & David Kline, *Rembrandts in the Attic: Unlocking the Hidden Value of Patents*, Harvard Business School Press, 2000, p. 45.
3 "Brands in a Bind," *Business Week*, August 28, 2000, pp. 234–8.
4 The Procter and Gamble Company, Annual Report 2000.

CHAPTER 6

1 "Intellectual Property Mall of Franklin Pierce Law Center, Intellectual Property Expected to be 'Practice of the Decade' According to New Survey," PR Newswire, June 15, 2000.

2 "Patent Wars," *Economist*, April 8, 2000, pp. 95–9.

3 Seth Shulman, *Owning the Future*, Houghton Mifflin, 1999.

4 *Red Herring*, No. 86, December 4, 2000, pp. 108–11.

5 Tom Blackett, *Trademarks*, Macmillan Business, 1998.

6 Richard Poynder (ed.), *Caught in a Web: Intellectual Property in Cyberspace*, Derwent Thomson Scientific, 2001.

7 See www.bustpatents.com for an up-to-date listing of major US patent damages awards.

8 "UK Overturns Viagra Patent," *Financial Times*, November 9, 2000; "Pfizer Statement on Viagra Use Patent Litigation in the United Kingdom," press release, November 8, 2000.

9 "Pfizer Statement on Viagra Use Patent Litigation in the United Kingdom," press release, November 8, 2000.

10 "BT sues Prodigy over US hyperlink patent," thestandard.com, December 18, 2000.

11 See www.bustpatents.com.

12 Kevin G. Rivette & David Kline, *Rembrandts in the Attic: Unlocking the Hidden Value of Patents*, Harvard Business School Press, 2000.

13 "USPTO Roundtable Scheduled to Discuss Issues, Solutions for Business Method Patents, *BNA Patent, Trademark & Copyright Daily*, July 5, 2000.

14 "Patent Nonsense," *Economist*, April 8, 2000, p. 99.

15 "Bezos-backed Site Puts Price on Patents," *E-commerce Times*, October 20, 2000.

16 Richard Behar, "Beijing's Phoney War on Fakes," *Fortune*, October 30, 2000.

CHAPTER 8

1 "Angry and Effective," Economist.com, September 23, 2000.

2 Seth Shulman, *Owning the Future*, Houghton Mifflin, 1999.

3 Charles Handy, "Is Your Company an Elephant or a Flea?," keynote speech, CIPD conference, Harrogate, October 27, 2000.

4 Seth Shulman, *Owning the Future*, Houghton Mifflin, 1999.

5 Hernando de Soto, *The Mystery of Capital*, Bantam Press, 2000.

6 "Patents and Patients," FT.com, February 17, 2001; "Science and

Profit," Economist.com, February 15, 2001.

7 "Venter Capital," *Red Herring*, June 2000, p. 296; "Patent Panic," *Red Herring*, July 2000, p. 203.

8 "Patent Panic," *Red Herring*, July 2000, p. 203.

9 "The Selfish Geneticist," *Financial Times*, December 30/31, 2000.

10 "Who Owns the Knowledge Economy?," *Economist*, April 8, 2000.

11 Naomi Klein, *No Logo*, Picador, 2000.

CHAPTER 9

1 United Brands Company (76/353/EEC).

CHAPTER 10

1 Stephen R. Covey, *7 Habits of Highly Effective People*, Simon & Schuster, 1999.

2 Kevin G. Rivette & David Kline, *Rembrandts in the Attic*, Harvard Business School Press, 2000.

3 Stephen C. Glazier, *Patent Strategies for Business*, Euromoney Publications, 1995.

4 H. Jackson Knight, *Patent Strategies for Researchers and Research Managers*, Wiley, 1996.

5 Philip Grubb, *Patents for Chemicals, Pharmaceuticals and Biotechnology*, Clarendon Press, 1999.

6 www.uspto.gov.

7 www.european-patent-office.org.

8 www.jpo.go.jp.

9 www.patent.gov.uk.

10 www.wipo.int.

11 www.aipla.org.

12 www.cipa.org.uk.

CHAPTER 11

1 Community Trade Mark Application No. 428870.

2 US trade mark application no. 74485223 in the name of Harley

Davidson Inc.

3 Notice of the WIPO Committee of Experts of the Nice Union Classification of Goods and Services on Restructuring of Class 42 to create three additional classes 43 to 45 effective January 1 2002.

4 Pfizer Ltd and another v. Eurofood Link (UK) Ltd, Decision of the Chancery Division of the UK High Court of Justice, 10 December 1999.

5 "Microsoft Can Overtake Coke as World's Most Valuable Brand," *Independent*, 19 July 2000; "Microsoft Tops Brand League," FT.com, 17 July 2000.

6 Per Mollerup, *Marks of Excellence: The History and Taxonomy of Trade Marks*, Phaidon Press, 1997.

7 "The Battle for Middle Earth, *Lord of the Rings'* Struggles Aren't Just Fantasy Anymore," *Red Herring*, April 15, 2001, p. 82.

8 Ipex, US Trade Mark Registration no. 2391356.

9 Ipex, UK Trade Mark Registration no. 2186782.

10 Phil Carpenter, *Ebrands*, Harvard Business School Press, 2000.

11 Martin Lindstrom & Tim Frank Andersen, *Brand Building on the Internet*, Kogan Page, 2000.

12 Scott Ward, Larry Light, & Jonathan Goldstine, "What High-Tech Managers Need to Know About Brands," *Harvard Business Review*, Jul–Aug 1999.

13 Marcel Corstjens & Marie Carpenter, "From Managing Pills to Managing Brands," *Harvard Business Review*, Mar–Apr 2000.

14 Susannah Hart & John Murphy (eds), *Brands: The New Wealth Creators*, Macmillan Business/Interbrand, 1998.

15 Tom Blackett, *Trademarks*, Macmillan Business/Interbrand, 1998.

16 Al Ries & Laura Ries, *The 22 Immutable Laws of Branding*, HarperCollins, 1998.

17 www.uspto.gov.

18 www.jpo.go.jp.

19 www.patent.gov.uk.

20 www.oami.eu.int.

21 www.wipo.int.

22 www.aipla.org.

23 www.itma.org.uk.

CHAPTER 12

1 "Sales of Music Singles Hit by Napster Effect," FT.com, April 19, 2001.
2 John Perry Barlow, "The Next Economy of Ideas: Will Copyright Survive the Napster Bomb? Nope but Creativity Will," *Wired*, October 2000.
3 Anthony B. Perkins, "Digital Content Wars: Can't We All Just Get Along?," *Red Herring*, December 18, 2000.
4 "Napster Subscription Fees Planned by Bertelsmann," FT.com, January 29, 2001; "And the Band Plays On," *Economist*, February 15, 2001.
5 Seth Godin, *Permission Marketing: Turning Strangers into Friends, and Friends into Customers*, Simon & Schuster, 1999.
6 Esther Dyson, *Release 2.0: A Design for Living in the Digital Age*, Broadway Books, 1997.
7 Richard Poynder (ed.), *Caught in a Web: Intellectual Property in Hyperspace*, Derwent Information, 2001.
8 Lesley Ellen Harris, *Digital Property: Currency of the 21st Century*, McGrawHill Ryerson, Ontario, 1998.

AFTERWORD

1 "Merck & Co. to Pay $620m for Genomics Company," FT.com, May 11, 2001.
2 Anthony B. Perkins, "Will the Real Monopolist Please Stand Up?," *Red Herring*, May 1/15, 2001.
3 "Xerox Outlines New Printing System," CBS.MarketWatch.com, May 3, 2001; "Xerox Focuses on Solutions and Services to Drive New Sources of Revenue," press release on xerox.com, May 1, 2001.
4 Thomas A. Stewart, *The Wealth of Knowledge: Working with Intellectual Capital*, Nicholas Brealey Publishing, 2002.
5 Ibid.
6 "What Is behind Microsoft's Attack on Open-source Software?," *Economist*, May 10, 2001.

LEGAL DISCLAIMER

V IRTUAL MONOPOLY AIMS TO PROVIDE A FRESH AND INNOVATIVE overview of how intellectual property is used in today's business world. In attempting to describe business trends with a broad brush, it is inevitable that some finer points of legal detail become lost. This book has not been written as legal opinion, and should not be read or used as such.

Intellectual property can be a complex area of law and you are advised to take professional legal advice relevant to any particular business matter in which you may engage. This book is no substitute for professional legal counsel, and the author accepts no legal responsibility for any actions taken by any reader.

Index